THE HISTORY OF THE SIEGE

POETRY BY

ERIC PANKEY

CODHILL PRESS

ALSO BY ERIC PANKEY

The Future Perfect: A Fugue

Owl of Minerva: Poems

Crow-Work: Poems

Reliquaries

THE HISTORY OF THE SIEGE

POETRY BY

ERIC PANKEY

CODHILL PRESS
NEW YORK • NEW PALTZ

CODHILL PRESS

codhill.com

THE HISTORY OF THE SIEGE
 First Edition.

Published in the United States of America

ISBN 978-1-949933-24-6
Library of Congress Control Number: 2023947629

Cover and Book Design by Jana Potashnik
BAIRDesign • bairdesign.com

CONTENTS

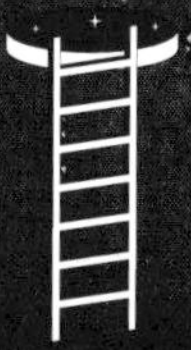

Too old to carry arms and fight like the others—

they graciously gave me the inferior role of chronicler
I record—I don't know for whom—the history of the siege

I am supposed to be exact but I don't know when the invasion began
two hundred years ago in December in September perhaps yesterday at dawn
everyone here suffers from a loss of the sense of time

—Zbigniew Herbert

Forever—is composed of Nows.

—Emily Dickinson

But the past is already here, and you are nursing some private project.

—John Ashbery

Finally, time is threadbare, a cast-off coat at the rag-merchant's.

—Pierre Reverdy

NO ONE TREATS YOU LIKE A MOTHER WHEN YOUR MOTHER IS DEAD

Seven or eight blossoms
On the little apple tree.
Barely a pie in the offing.

Only yesterday, my mother was a fifth-grader bareback upon a donkey in Arkansas. Her house has a coal chute and a laundry chute: gravity the technology of the day. If she leans too far to pick a buttercup, she might fall off the donkey. The name of the donkey? Whatever she calls it, it responds. Already in spring, she thinks of autumn. There's the memory of the sound of sparrow wings in a hedge. Water in the creek working around rocks. Her father, his right eye a little clouded, dimmer than the left, is a widower. A widower in a town of widows, but he will not remarry. She calls him Floyd, which is his given name. The past, unlike the future, is surround by a narrow margin of silence. The future is accompanied as always with sparse, plaintive music, as if to announce *something is about to happen.* The *something* unclear until it happens. A little dust whirls up, then disappears like a bit of advice from a soothsayer. *Lux. Lumina.* Wavelengths are absorbed or reflected. A thunderstorm interrupts the afternoon. Late summer, her garden thrives, begun with bargained-for cuttings from this widow or that. She likes the shadows cast by the lace curtains onto the pale of the pine kitchen floor. Someday, she thinks, I'll write it all down—not to remember, but so as not to forget.

I STAYED ALL NIGHT IN THE CABIN

I count and measure the distance thunder travels. I have lived here longer than I have lived anywhere but it does not yet feel like home. I forgot to take a number upon entering. I pulled a small nest of hair that was not mine from the brush. I failed to notice that *sacrifice* had been replaced by *ritual eating*. I stayed in the cabin all night, but there was no lightning at the Lightning Field.

THE AFTERLIFE

In the afterlife, there are no names, no need for registers, no attendance-taking. One can be neither tardy nor late. One has always arrived early. The seat one wished for awaits, and no one occupies the seat ahead. No one near you talks after the theater lights dim. Without a name, one must be introduced anew at each gathering and receives the welcome, hospitality, and honor of a newcomer. One need not worry about arriving perfectly prepared. If one is to take something with a grain of salt, a grain of salt will be provided. In the afterlife, a deep, hidden meaning never threatens the secure tranquility of simple and ingenious things. The slow art of forgetting occupies what passes here for time.

THE DRESS

This could be the dress you sewed in ninth grade, cut from fragile, tea-stained pattern papers pinned to scrap fabric. This could be the dress the intruder wore when caught on the survelience footage. This could be the dress your mother set aside to give away to the Good Will. This dress, as thin as shed snakeskin, is perfect for porch-sitting on a hot summer night. A prototype of *the dress,* the dress, in its complex modesty, neither cloaks nor reveals.

NATIVE AS YOU ARE TO NOTHING

At midnight, time thins like wisps of clouds over mountains, snags like wool on barbed wire. At midnight, the unforeseen holds its tongue. At midnight, the soul is as empty as a cicada husk. At midnight, neither divination nor happenstance will suffice. At midnight, the half-moon of a grub stirs in cold clay.

How quick the fox at midnight! How rain falls only on the tip of its tail!

Midnight is to the day what a cellar is to a house, a dark place, dank, where things are set down and forgotten. Native as you are to nothing, you are familiar with how cluttered nothingness can be. There is no need to document the ephemeral, to theorize the materiality of shadow. Feel free to look away. The dead stars, after all, hung upon their hooks, begin to look like an ill-lit abattoir.

THE ENTREPRENEUR

The day the war ends, he recalls each thin curl of maple that unfurled before the hand plane. He recalls the sawdust, tacky with humidity, as it fell from the ripsaw's blade. He recalls the shellac's soporific vapors. He waits now for the day the soldiers will return home in need of the crutches and prosthetic limbs he has crafted. At the start of the war, a mere carpenter, he had thought of specializing in coffin-making, but word of surprising advances in battlefield medicine made him think again.

AS A THUNDERHEAD GATHERS

A magnetic field, a force field, a field guide. How *soldier* becomes *solder* and *solid,* the soul the size of a seed, the size of a tick. How the humid air condenses upon it; how the soul, free from flesh, glistens with dew. The starlings are startled: out of sorts, out of socket. Watercress, water crest, the water's rest. A cotton dress on a line in Rogers, Arkansas dries as a thunderhead gathers. The newer paved roads are not on the map. How the earth rotates on its axis while in revolution. The *ax is,* the *axes.* Follow the fallow field. *Tip your hat brim if you see an atomic flash,* her father advises, *to protect yourself against the fallout.*

WITH WORDS

When the frequency with which a ghost shimmers is slowed, it becomes visible. What then is the tense it resides in?

: :

As I kneeled and spoke in tongues at the revival at the First Baptist Church of Raytown in 1974, I could taste the salt of shame, the bitter of stammer and blather, the cloy and sweet of reckless surrender.

: :

A word comes to mind and is lost. Words are such simple tools, and, like tools, easily misplaced.

: :

The past nags like a bone spur. While I was away, the future arrived. If only forgiveness were as easy as forgetfulness.

: :

I wished my father dead for so long and then he died as if my wishing made it so. Now with words I attempt to raise him from the dead.

: :

The poem aware of my eavesdropping, lowers its voice. Whispers. Speaks a language composed entirely of vowels.

MY MOTHER SET THE HOUSE ON FIRE

My mother set the house on fire. An artist, she let an unfiltered Camel smolder on the sofa arm until, from the smoke, a flame flared up. She called the work "The Aftermath"—charred lath, singed pink insulation, and the rafters' embers sputtering out on the square concrete slab upon which the house once stood.

She filmed me—six-years-old—in my pj's and slippers amid the ruin with a bucket of water slung in each arm and titled the award-winning three-channel video installation "Fireproof."

When family services were called, they said she had the maternal instinct of a recluse spider. That's when I went to live with my father, a circus fire breather. I slept on parking-lot pavement beneath his 1959 Streamline Travel Trailer inside my very own emptied box of Diamond Strike-on-the-Side 250 Count Large Kitchen Matches, which as you know, have been America's match company since 1881.

INFILTRATION & SEEPAGE

Water moves through topographies. A river system maps the descent. So much forgetting intermingled: a daytime star, a dissonant harmony, the ordinary bled of its strangeness. With only fog to bathe in, I prefer to enact my grief in private, to not be seen as *wreckage come upon,* what a hollow holds, or lets slip: a glimpse of the unknown, the unknowing. I understand the arrangement, the rush to conclusion, to the infinite regress. A river moves in and through time, becoming. The space—undefined, insubstantial, disquieting—precludes entry. By way of a scope—a peephole or an aperture—I reiterate the distance, the distances for an audience of empty chairs. If not aforementioned, would time even exit?

EXAGGERATED GESTURES

A month (or is it two?) into the pandemic, one day is not the same as the next, but the distinction between them is quite subtle: the five minutes of bright sun yesterday between cloudbursts, the sudden racket of the crows' call and response. Neighbors, who have politely ignored one another for years, have taken to waving, to acknowledging at last something shared, even if it is a predicament. We smile behind our masks, exaggerate our gestures so as to be understood at a safe distance. *Look,* we seem to say, *we are alike—alive, that is.*

A STOP AT WILLOUGHBY: *TWILIGHT ZONE*, SEASON ONE, EPISODE 30

Lightning all night but rain fell only on the mountain. What is that something withheld, but now forgotten, a degree or two shy of true north? From the train window: a little island with a willow at its center. You keep moving, an hour ahead of daylight. Thunderheads ride the horizon like galleons. A fire smothered with the ash of previous fires. By noon tomorrow, wasps will halo the figs. You hold the raveled thread of the present. As before, stillness bristles. *Maybe,* you think, leaning toward yes, *I'll get off at Willoughby.*

A WEATHERED LADDER

A shutter creaks in wind. Mute as I am, without one word to name this or that, I walk each day the circular path around the hilltop town. If I go clockwise or counterclockwise, I seem to have taken the uphill path. Halfway, I seek shade, not fruit, in an unkempt orchard. Propped against a cherry tree, a weathered ladder leads to the sky. When I return from my walk an hour later, whichever way I turn the key in the door is the wrong way. And so, I do the opposite. By then, interrupted by the key's rattling, you have opened the door.

CELADON

Evening settles as subtle salt light in each window. The first star appears unnoticed. A child notes rust's slow progress on a drainpipe. Moves a snail back to where its moonlit celadon trail began.

: :

She woke to find the pupa of a rare butterfly lodged beneath the skin of her wrist. Its rhythmic shimmer like a celadon pulse.

: :

Celadon ceramic glaze—pale, jade-green, transparent—originated at the start of the Northern Song Dynasty and is commonly called *greenware* nowadays.

: :

The maid servant, cloaked in an elaborate celadon silk dress, attends her mistress at the beheading and carries away on an ornate silver tray Holofernes' head.

: :

In his notebook, a list of color names that never made it into poems: *titian, bisque, puce, fulvous, smalt, celadon, damask, gamboge, bittersweet, feldgrau,* and *jasper.*

NEARSIGHTED

Over on the far point, a scrim of light divides the various darks. A chain, crutched between two points, that droops and peaks like a child's drawing of waves. Through the slack heat it blurs and flickers. From this distance, I cannot tell if it's a string of party lights strung all along the cliff's edge, or points to mark a greater length: scattered lights left on in the white frame houses the coastline shelves. It would be dangerous to walk that road at this hour, to tempt the cars that wind the narrow bends—high beams buffered by fog—or the drunken boys looking to break the boredom.

A scream pulled me from sleep, a scream all too near. The dank heat takes on mass. In it sounds double and ring: noises are like thrown voices. My slept broken, entered, cannot be reclaimed, so I stand: meek voyeur, bad witness, with my glasses off, unsure what I am looking at or for. Someone crosses the marsh. The flashlight bobs as he runs. Pointed down, it pools, elongates. But the only sound is a slosh. A rush of grasses. There is no other scream.

Who knows if that runner is fleeing the scene? If there is a scene? Tonight, no moon shines. No sliver drags a chalky edge. Nearsighted, I stare out at the fringe of lights—some shimmering, some as blank as planets—and squint. The whole thing flares like a burning net, a trap sprung each night and empty.

POCKETSIZE NOTEBOOK WITH A BLACK ELASTIC STRAP TO HOLD IT CLOSED

In the dream, I complain how “dream” is often excluded from general lists of time-based media. But no one listens, and by “no one” I mean the passersby in the rain-dimmed light. I am looking for a dry place where I might shelter and add this dream to the dream journal I keep thinking would be useful to keep—as a source for poems, say, or to figure out what is nagging at me, or merely as a way to say I write daily, when, if truth be told, I do not. I have not written anything since I bought the pocketsize black notebook with a black elastic strap to hold it closed. In the dream, I am certain that the notebook itself is the cause, the reason why I cannot seem to put pencil to paper, cannot rub two words together and make the slightest of sparks. I find a seat by the door in a coffee shop I did not know existed. At every table a person is writing in a pocketsize black notebook with a black elastic strap. When I open my notebook, I find a single line in my own hand I do not remember having written: *A pillar of fire is a foretaste.*

THE RIVER STILL RAGGED WITH ICE FLOES

The woodcutter opened the wolf's belly with a well-honed axe, but found no grandmother, no girl, and no home-baked goodies. The wolf moaned, "Why did you gut me so? I told you that you would find nothing." The woodcutter filled the hollowed beast with gravel and stone, and sewed the wound shut with a tangle of fishing line. Before pushing the creature into the river still ragged with ice floes, the woodcutter asked, "Given the chance, might you have devoured a child, her grandma, and a basket of tasty treats?" The wolf, before it sank, replied, "I admit I am a wolf."

REDEMPTION SONG

The story goes that Seth returned to Eden in search of a branch from the Tree of Life. The angel, so moved by his plea, opened the gate, and not only offered, but cut the highest branch with his fiery sword. The tree's sap sang out as it boiled and sealed the wound.

After he returned home, Seth's followers huddled around the gift of the cutting, which had rooted and grown into a tree overnight. They admired the magic of the tree, in flower and fruit at the same moment: the delicate white of the petals, the red-streaked throats disappearing into the green wood, the ripe fruit which they pulled easily away from its hard seed stone.

They passed the flesh from person to person, some commenting on its sweetness, some on its bitterness, some on its hint of salt. Seth listened to the fire he'd built: its damp wood whined; he watched his children asleep there by the flames.

When one child woke crying from a dream, he picked her up and slowly rocked her. He hummed what he could remember of a song his mother had once sung: the simple music served its purpose.

EURYDICE

We see her in the moment of her vanishing. She is there, then not. Of course, she has no agency. He turns. He turns back. And we see her. Gone. Vanished in a moment. And without agency. He turns and, because of his turning, she is swept back into the dark. Vanished, she is not there. Was she ever? Even for a moment? He turns, surprised to find her not there. The story would not be a story without that turn. Without her lack of agency. He turns in the dark and watches her vanish. Or, as he, the poet, would put it:

She slips away—a frail shadow at a threshold overwhelmed
By lightning: banished, cast out, as quick as viper's venom—

WHICH IS TO SAY

The ghost of Don Giovanni breaks and enters and finds what he finds in each house: a table set for a meal still unprepared. The beds made. Neatly folded clothes in the chest of drawers. Nothing out of the ordinary on the bookshelves. Books he had read as a young man, books that had seemed strange and provocative, now seem tame. When he has time to read, he prefers the character-driven to the picaresque, long passages of thought that do not advance the plot, but rather the argument of the novel.

Even as a ghost, he is and was a man, which is to say, a brute, a monster.

He kept secrets about the lies he told. He lied to keep his secrets. Each night he breaks into another house and is relieved to find no one at home.

LILITH

Upside down, spider-like on the wall, she looks up at us and meets our eyes. Her beauty, an unintended consequence, terrifies. Neither echo nor shadow. Singular. There is for her, in leaving no trace, no path of return. The fog lingers. The fog dissipates. Distance is brought close: the still riverbend, the web dew-jeweled. The present—continuous, persistent—is *present*. She has no patience for that which comes after, for the belated. She sees us as we are: replicas. Creatures of darkness, distilled from light's residue: shovelfuls of soot and grit suspended in sluggish, waxy tallow.

A GRID OVER THE DEBRIS FIELD

Although they broke up she went on living in the house with him, calculating the ratio of risk to return by placing a grid over the debris field. She must have misheard him: *a tree made entirely of prose.* To him she pointed out *the downed power lines in the downpour.* Winds shiver in the trees and are what dreams are to a mind: random firings made sense of and upon awakening forgotten. *Does dust gather on still water,* he asked in an effort at affection, *and if so how soon before it dissolves or sinks and settles?* The sky blues in the distance. The ocean on one side, the mountain on the other, compose a space of habitation. She awaits a market correction, pieces their past together like a quilt. By *desire of the other,* did she mean the *other's* desire or *her* desire *for* an other? With wind within them, the trees fill and empty and like a heart are never filled, never emptied wholly.

THE FORGOTTEN HOLDALL

I booked an adjacent room. The floor plan suggested the space of experience, not the experience of space. Her room had a view, both fugitive and sublime. From my room, all extraneous detail had been removed except for an atlas of stray thoughts. I thought *north* meant *up*. There were other subsequent failures. I wore my shirt inside out: the seams' bad stitching on view as I walked along the towpath by the river and looked up. From the balcony, she enacted a kind of sign language, variations upon gestures one might mistake for dance. Neither seduced nor repulsed, I watched, entangled in ambiguity, in the rendering's implied violence. I should be in a cab, I thought. I should be on my way to the train station or airport or pier where a ship is departing, but my holdall, for some reason, waits outside her door to be picked up: a slumped teabag that weeps dark tannins into the ornate carpet.

INTERFERENCE PATTERN

Time, although continuous, deceives us with its notion of *now.* Regret, as always, belated. Each scene—rehearsed, enacted, workshopped, and revised—is the length of a day, an hour, an absence set in motion by a gesture of erasure: a damp gray slate. Rain on a shale outcrop. Rain as an unexpected foreclosure. A gap opens and the visible is absorbed into such a pewter. How many different temporalities combine to equal the past? How does touch translate the light night inhales and holds? Watched from a distance, the house windows go dark one by one. What remains? An abridgement. An axe taken to a frozen sea. Rocks circled nest-like to define a space. We are asked to put it back like we found it, to exit before the toll. Of course, something surrounds the *around-which.* Of course, we are aghast at the horror of *no-likeness,* of each thing distinct: a velvet of charcoal, the cold fixed form of lava, the camouflage of big data. To forestall time, on which night must fall, a ghost condenses out of air: a coherent mirage, a message without recipient, a losing hand dealt. What does a façade harbor? The raw materials of notes? The collaborations and interventions? A mass that turns out to be a muddle of intersecting lines? A loom of silhouettes? Bare, brittle branches? A blister is easily rubbed up. The net, pulled in, grows heavier as it surfaces, sloughs water. In the future, we will speak in the present tense and feel nothing like dislocation, only the wire's frayed end and a glitchy disharmony: a hitch. A snag. A malfunction. A sleight of hand. Transubstantiation.

RECENTLY RECOVERED PAGES FROM *THE COMPLETE LIST OF EVERYTHING*

A stand of birches. A clutter of grave goods. The compensation of levity. A theremin as a stand-in for birdsong. Pulleys and levers. Indigenous cannibals. Lightning's musket-flash. A wracked ship. A provocation or cure. A dumpster fire. The graphic notation of music. The end of enigma. Footfalls without echo. A backward glance. An untethered horse. A billboard advertising itself as a place to advertise. The prior state. An atlas of anatomy. River clay. A monument to entropy. The error introduced while editing a text. The past impinged upon by the present. A cigar box guitar. A do-over to redo. The tents of the Red Cross. A hand-sewn fascicle. The endgame. A quarantine. Asemic writing. Gouges, mauls, and plummets. A punch line. An enslaved spirit. Mars black and lamp black. A complete list of everything (as of yet incomplete). The interior chamber of a camera obscura. Illicit trade and trafficking. A remix of the original. An argument in favor of the use of anachronisms. A caustic solution of lye water. That old narrative of katabasis and anabasis. The frosty white face of a nuthatch. A cello's scroll. Hand tools. Disambiguation. A bolete, a puffball, and a stinkhorn. The blue gills of a white cap mushroom. Straw spun to gold. A foil. An enemy. Either end of the continuum. The treachery of images. Albacore, alewife, alligator gar. The omen of a partial solar eclipse. The live version of Joy Division's "Transmission." A postcard from Barcelona. Ancillary work. A clear-cut ridge. The beautiful bird revealing the unknown to a pair of lovers. The nostalgia of the reactionary. Lead crystal. A benevolent

>

coven. The killing fields. The killing floor. The killdeer. Every interplay of light and shade. Snakefruit. Soursop. Mouse melon. A trick of the eye. The phenomenology of dust. A slightly forced perspective. Eminent domain. An arrowless quiver. The interval in between. Windborne seeds. A rift. The affront of a taboo. The rabbit as trickster. A bonefolder. An egg balanced on an anvil. A bat-eared fox. A black lemur. A bush dog. A foothold on the rung. A fugue for woodwinds. Kiln. Crucible. Cauldron. Yucca fibers. A crisp. A cobbler. A pie. An unauthorized biography. Hair loose from a braid. Memory submerged in water. An open wound. Debunked conspiracy theories. Cloud chamber. Chamber music. Andirons (also called firedogs). Noun meaning *one who is highly sensitive to clichés*. Ill-intentioned ghosts. Random access memory. The improbable. The Industrial Revolution. Sludge build-up. A river silted in. An insinuated preamble. *Objets d'art.* Star anise. A naïve melody. A doomsday malaise. Newfangledness. Figure 63. Blind Willie Johnson's scratchy recording of "I Just Can't Keep from Crying." A flock of clothespins perched on the line. A foxglove. A shark's eye. Illegible inscription. A dream's function. A Clovis point. The tabled motion. A bog as a site to conceal a crime. Evaded taxes. An ocean trench. Basalt, granite, and rhyolite. A lute out of tune. More of a snag than a glitch. The Gospel according to Mary. Stolen passport. Calligraphic brushstrokes. Terra incognita. A smoke ring. The structure of an event. Cold Mountain. The unsent letter. The night watch. A thorn thicket. The *the*. Sleet. A marooned polar bear adrift on ice. The grinding pace of light years.

ASH-GRIT

Without you, even the silence is depleted. Shadows, out of proportion to their objects, gather like standing water in the hollows. Once, my heart was a bow of tough yew wood. Once my heart was a balanced arrow, its four flight-feather's sealed with spruce gum. Without you, my days are a ramshackle shelter of sticks, a piano left to molder on a mountain of rain. Without you, I am ash-grit on a whitewashed wall.

SHALLOW FORD IN THE RIVER

A man washes a horse in the shallow ford of a river. The man says, "Lift your leg." And the horse lifts its leg. The water runs swiftly past. This point on the map is marked *always,* the midpoint between *arrival* and *departure.*

TO RENDER THE IMPRESSION OF PERSPECTIVE

As I come out of the glare into the shade of the canyon's circumambient walls, the cool, hewn from rock, startles me. The only petroglyph I find: *Mark & Denise 1979* and two rough-drawn interlocking hearts scraped onto rock with rock. Above the dry cobbled creek: silver-leaf flash of dragonflies. Raw caws of ravens. Skitter of rock and gravel over the bank. Once, not far from here, an angel guided a plow and rain followed like seed from a sower's hand. I have assumed the drawing is of hearts, but one could see a Venn diagram, say, or two apples, one slightly in front of the other, to render the impression of perspective.

LOST

The boy is not lost but looks for something lost. On each floor: a corridor of numbered doors accessed by a stairwell. There are no stairs. The boy must rig a rope. Sisal rubs and burns his hands as he climbs. No. Not something lost but rather left behind. Something far too heavy, far too cumbersome with which to shimmy down the length of the rope, which of course will be cut down when he returns burdened to the stairwell with whatever it is he came to reclaim. His flight left a half-hour ago with a single empty seat. It is after checkout time. His father will be charged for another night.

THE CALL-IN SHOW

I have broken radio silence, but dare not open the lead-lined blackout curtains for better reception. The signal scrambles within the wire cage's grid, distorted by subatomic particles, by decay patterns, and by the folds of gravity where one universe is subducted beneath another. I'm a first time caller, long time listener. If you can hear me out there, I'll take my answer off the air.

BURIED FOR NOW

in memory of my brother

An island is a body surround by water; a peninsula is something quite different, as is an inlet or isthmus; that said, the noontime objects hid their shadows; spoons in the drawer slept the sleep of spoons; I cannot remember the words or the silences but have a vague recollection of the weather that linked them, floods and fallen facades; the answers came too easily, you said, as if someone were feeding me my lines from backstage; how long the smoke hung after rain, the bonfire smoke, the bonfire of ladders; even now, the fugue ache, the seven curses that turned back seven winds; the years continue to float on their sides like blue gill; your death certificate remains under a pile of papers on my desk, buried for now, easily exhumed; the stationary ran out, so I wrote on the motel room wall with chalk; the chalk ran out, so I wrote with water on the carpet; I did not bother to turn into the spin, my face in the rearview an apt self-portrait as the ditch approached; the willow lashes at the wind, the wind lashes back; the exchange is untenable, is wreckage, is fraught, is over for now; an island is a body surrounded by water, a peninsula is something quite different, as is an inlet or isthmus; that said, I was not a good brother.

A TRAUMA

What am I to make, in the dream, of the risen Jesus' wounds—blunt piercings, raw lash marks, blood-beaded thorn-pricks, a deep gash in his side that does not and will not fester, nor draw flies—the witness of his wounds, a dead man alive who does not quite resemble himself, or at least is not recognized by those who should know him, who expect to find a tortured and executed body in a pit or cave, adorned in a three-day stink like a beggar's shawl, picked apart, perhaps, by dogs, and not this, this animated man moving among them speaking in riddles? On second glance, or because of his admonition, or that this is just how magic works in stories, they see him for who he is or was, a strange man among them speaking in riddles. Like his followers, I have been through a trauma in the dream (from the Greek, *traumatikos,* meaning "pertaining to a wound") which I can accept or deny, treat as the end of one tale, or the beginning of another. A story that moved among them, that moves through me, like an infection.

THE INVISIBLE MAN

The invisible man courts anonymity and leaves his sunglasses and a heap of unrolled bandages upon the floor. He grows tired of the fraught drama of sleight of hand, tired of the shadow labyrinth set down by the window's elaborate leadwork.

To ward off harm, he takes a plaster cast of the interior of the small coat closet, places it in his foyer, and cloaks it in a black velvet skin. The closet's cramped dark, embodied now as a positive space, seems to him as he walks around it a monolith, a heavenly mansion.

BALANCED ON THE CHAIR'S BACK LEGS

No one slipped you a mickey. No one stole you from your crib and left behind a changeling. The X-ray glasses you sent away for *did* work: you just didn't know what you were looking at. You are safe in front of the curtain, lead lined as it is: the real violence happens offstage. If bored, spin the night's tedium into a thread; tie both ends of the thread into slipknots. Slip one knot over an incisor. Slip the other over a doorknob. If you feel dizzy, a chair will be provided. Lean back and balance on the chair's back legs. Close your eyes. Relax. The shade a prayer casts lasts longer than the prayer.

FROM THE GET-GO

I could tell from the start that the whole business would come to no good, no good for those who set the plan in motion and no good for those who found themselves in its crosshairs. That said, it wasn't a bad plan, but like all plans had its downsides and well, we were among those who stood to get hurt, to take the brunt, to have our asses handed to us. I didn't care, but she hired me to do a job and so I thought I ought to get it done: an odd code that seems only to come into play where a redhead is involved. My mother was a redhead and I imagine it all goes back to that, some memory or moment, some glimpse that affixed in my too-young brain something strange that perhaps years on the shrink's couch might untangle. Like I said, the case was doomed from the get-go and yet I cannot seem to move it ahead, to let the plot plod along, to let each effect hold hands with its cause. We are here. Or rather, there: a beachside motel where the towels never dry by the next day, where the maid tracks in as much sand as she sweeps up. Three or four days have gone by, and we wait to make the exchange, a duffle full of cash for ransom. The kidnappers are smart. They sent us here and will probably send us elsewhere before the whole thing ends with her sister dead, or her sister convicted of trying to trick her out of the cash. The sister is a redhead too and that makes me nervous, because often in these stories she is a brunette or a bleached blonde; she is different, even if a twin, from her sister and somehow, I am supposed to intuit which one

I should trust, rather than merely trusting, taking orders like some cabdriver with the whole night and all the city's streets ahead of me. I know you don't know me from Adam and why should you care how this all turns out, but since I have your ear let me ask you something. Why all that pomade on your hair? Do you think that looks good? And what about the stink? The ransom note, you know, smells just like that—waxy, a little burnt, some cooking oil gone rancid, pea soup left on a low burner all night.

AS IN ANY MARRIAGE

In the sequel, the Fifty-Foot Woman marries the Incredible Shrinking Man. For their love and its attendant mysteries, alphabets and enumerations prove inadequate. The words they speak ill-fit their objects: the miniature *and* the outsized. She cannot help but see the big picture. His hummingbird heart—at high idle, silent to others—rattles away in his ribs. She tells bad jokes, like the one about the dog that ran away with the flea circus. To him, fleas are no laughing matter. As in any marriage, concessions are made: brine pits and barren places must do until they can afford a home of their own. He has a shady past. She has a deadpan wit. He finds her obtuse. She finds him among the crumbs. They argue over minutia and the sublime. Long ago they suspended their disbelief. They see the other as one sees the self in a mirror: familiar, if inelegant—opaque one moment, translucent the next. For those drawn to this story out of prurient interest, rest assured: their bodies are a medium of exchange, asymmetrical forms that fit, despite logic, and with more than a little trepidation.

EIGHT PREPARATORY DRAWINGS

THE HAIRDRESSER

Every Saturday, her grandmother went to the hairdresser. At church on Sunday, she would say, "Grandma, your hair looks amazing. Did you do something new to it?" Her grandmother would blush and with a shaky hand reach up to her hair-sprayed hair, but not touch it, and say, "I'm so glad you noticed."

HER FIRST HUSBAND

Everyone advised her against marrying her first husband, to which she would reply, "You don't know him like I do." Her first husband bought a motorcycle with her student loan. Her first husband, when, at the end of the month, things got tight, would siphon gas from the neighbors' cars. Her first husband often asked, "Have I ever hit you?" To which she had to reply, "No."

HER FACE

She did not like to go anywhere without her makeup. "I don't have my face on yet," she would say when a friend stopped by early to pick her up. "You look fine," her friend would say. "That," she would say back, "is sweet of you. But I can't have my friends lying to me." And would keep her friend waiting until her face was on.

>

CUP AND SAUCER

Her father, when he wanted more coffee at breakfast, would rattle his cup against the saucer and her mother would get up from the table, fetch the coffee pot and fill his cup. As a *thank you* he would say *uhm* without lifting his eyes from his morning newspaper. “May I be excused?” she would ask, and her mother would say, “Don’t ask me; ask your father.” Her father would say *uhm*.

DARK MATTER

She never told anyone about the anger, like a fist of slag where her heart should be and all the flesh around it bruised, inflamed, scraped, infected. A sourceless anger. An anger without a target. Over time, the anger took on more mass, more gravity, transmuting from anger to rage. And at those times, she imagined that all the dark matter in the universe was lodged there behind her ribs. How could she stand? How could she take a step and move through the world with such a sublime and concentrated fury at her core? But she could. And she did.

LONE TREE

In the 80s, growing up in Lone Tree, Iowa, she read in the paper of the farm foreclosures, the migration of failed farmers away from the land to the big cities six hours away in all directions: Minneapolis, Chicago, St. Louis, Kansas City, the falling price of corn, the rash of suicides. Her father, a large animal vet, spent his days driving around Johnson County, offering his skills to many who could not pay. Her father was fond of whistling and at that time, she recalls, he often whistled the old Stephen Foster song "Hard Times." She was listening to Springsteen's pared-back album *Nebraska* then. Her mother asked if the two of them knew any happy music. Her mother preferred to perform happiness, even if she was not. Her mother was from What Cheer, Iowa, a former coal town, just south in Keokuk County. Today, April 6, 2023, she looks up the weather in Lone Tree, Iowa online and it is 36°F (2°C), Wind W at 14 mph. and is she is glad she left that harsh climate behind long ago. Cold, her father used to say, as a witch's tit.

PROBABILITY

She had not thought of it, at first, as a rape, as rape. But what else to call it? Through the short length of it, she wondered what she had communicated by way of her surprise and wordlessness, what silent permission he felt he had been given and had gladly taken. During the second rape (a different man, a different decade) she had fought back with all her strength, clawed at his eyes, bit into his bicep, kneed his balls, screamed. The hospital, the police station, the courthouse, and acquittal followed. She understands well the world around her. She cannot help but consider the possibility of, the probability of, a third rape.

THE OLD HYMNS

Her second husband's first marriage had fallen apart after the death of their child shortly after its birth. He and

>

his first wife had struggled for years to stay together, but the lost child eclipsed all else in their relationship. Now, when she and her second husband decided not to have children (she was thirty-nine by then and he forty-five) they felt a great relief at the decision, a lightness they had not expected. They would spend long Sunday mornings at the art museum, taking their time over new exhibitions and the permanent collection. They tried with great sincerity and honesty to explain to one another exactly what the work before them made them think and feel. She preferred *Annunciations.* He preferred *Descents from the Cross.* Both, in their earlier lives, had been believers. He treated that belief now with a kind of nostalgia and had for it an ache that felt warm. She had attended church with her grandmother and there had learned to sing and read music. She still loved the old hymns but was bothered by the notion of a blood sacrifice, never mind the divinity of Jesus. Although he knew he ought not to, he asked if her attraction to *Annunciations* suggested a longing for motherhood. "No," she countered, "I have always wanted to be visited by angels."

THE CHECKPOINT

The moon hoards the little light that falls upon it. To see it is to trespass. The signs are posted, and that slack length of uncoiled barbwire was meant to keep you on the other side. The password you scribbled down on your palm is out of date. It does not matter. The checkpoint guard has abandoned his post. Like you, he is where he should not be, squinting to see something lit by a sullen, threadbare, secondhand light.

WITHOUT LIKENESS

With a slight turn of your head, the margin becomes the center: a fugitive elsewhere, a fleeting something felt but not articulated. Is the project a ruin, or a structure not yet complete? A glimpse where you find yourself? How do you tolerate the tenuous, the diffuse, with fire as an element of grammar? The forest conceals a lake, the lake a cave, the cave an underground river: each bend the arc of *scatter*. So much forgetting intermingled as you rush to conclusions: the past eclipsed by immediate concerns, albeit temporarily. The uprisings and revolutions mutate into late night dance parties for which few, yourself included, are willing to break curfew. Those remaining at dawn are dispersed easily by street sweepers.

THE OLD DEVIL IN THE TREE

Shyness, not modesty, afflicts the Old Devil in the Tree. The deceptive light makes the dark appear limitless. Easily mistaken for the Boy with a Cloud for a Head, or some orientalist's dream of Salome, the Old Devil in the Tree knows little of the history of cruelty. He arrived by way of a slash in a cyclone fence; spent his formative years trapped as a spirit in a tree burl; watched too much Cinéma Vértité; collected banal curios at truck stops.

The Old Devil in the Tree is not even his *real* name, but one of many heteronyms without much fixity or hold. He enjoys the vague comfort of tidying-up; could use some more silence to breach the noise, more of yesterday's muted half-light: grainy, staticky, and permeable. He appreciates the privilege bestowed upon a curated object, the clean enclosure of the vitrine, but attends the gallery openings primarily for the complementary valet parking.

THE ENCOUNTER

Light narrows to fit the crack in the canopy, only to widen and pool on the duff and underbrush, to drip like wax from the stag's eighteen-point rack. The stag, neither threat nor transport, shakes its head as if to answer a yes or no question with *yes* and *no,* and shreds the moth-thick air to an even dustier moonlight.

FEEDBACK & INTERFERENCE

Chamber music piped into a gas chamber, ghostly, barely-there; feedback and interference; the ping of sonar; a sin of omission; a prophecy unfulfilled; an anachronism; the beheading's audience; a consonant obscured; a vowel swallowed; an image washed-out; a salvaged slave ship; CCTV footage of the kidnapping; the jittery market; the undisclosed sum; the accrued interest.

NOVEL MICROBES IN THE ICE MELT

In the nearest shelter, asylum seekers crowd the couch, which sits mid-room: a raft awaiting a shipwreck. They are afflicted with a sleep disorder now linked to a deficit in starlight. The water released from the reactor pool does not glow but stinks like something washed up from the benthic zone. The coincident present is as unstable as ever. It flees yet is infected with a precarious inertia that they have read about in the memorandum of regret. Each retracing of the circle amplifies its imperfections. There are novel microbes in the ice melt. As the asylum seekers wait, they are surprised by the loom's clatter, by the paperwork, and by the sheer tedium of due diligence. *If something is boring,* John Cage says, *after two minutes, try it for four. If it is still boring, then eight. Then sixteen. Then thirty-two. Eventually one discovers that it is not boring at all.* They are released at last on their own recognizance. The subsidized rental, they are pleased to learn, "is not in the flood zone."

TO NO ONE IN PARTICULAR

Bob Dylan forgets that we have met several times, so I am not surprised that he does not look at me when I sit next to him at the diner's counter. He nudges my paper napkin and flatware toward me to create a little more space for himself as he eats his pie. The waitress shakes her head at me, meaning *leave him alone.* But I am curious about the ending of "Love Minus Zero/No Limits," in particular why the beloved is compared to a raven and not a crow (is it, for instance, a question of syllable count?) to which he answers, quoting, I am almost certain, Xenophanes, or some other ancient Greek, "Ethiopians make their gods black and snub-nosed and Thracians red-haired and blue-eyed." He pushes his plate away and rises to leave, and says to no one in particular, "The peach lacks a certain something. I would recommend the rhubarb." Perhaps that too is a quote, but the source eludes me.

THE BOREDOM THAT PRECEDES THE RAPTURE

Stripped of ritual, your gathering takes on the mood of a dinner party at which you are neither guest nor host. Stewed turnips weep into the mashed potatoes. The cod is undercooked. You are about to speak your mind, but the words shimmy and dangle before your eyes like three or four wasps inside a revival tent. The woman next to you complains of a feather lodged in her heart. Her husband argues that memory, like an echo, diminishes over distance. You notice the pencil lines on the wall, which once marked their child's changing height, have been painted over. Outside: blue nocturnal shadows, red twiggy remains of shrubs above snow. With each click of the View-Master, the scene changes: the dining room displaced by a thicket of whispers. By hearsay. By heresy.

LAST RADIO PLAYING

This is the silver skinned from a mirror. This is an hour's tedium in a motel room mistaken for ennui. This is the dream in which I am falling. This is the fallacy of gravity: more hindsight than discernment, more vortex than maelstrom. Rain like four walls holds incense smoke within the temple. Gnosis is tested and measured in the medium of language, which itself cannot be wholly trusted. This is the temporary configuration of meanders and migratory paths. This is, Bob Dylan sings, *the last temptation, the last account, last time you might hear the sermon on the mount, last radio playing.*

WITHOUT MYSTERY

What is there to do in such a small village but walk about, take in the views again—wildflowers in the siege wall's chinks, the restored church and wrought iron belfry, or down valley: the tilled fields, orchards, and vineyards—or to say *good day* to the shopkeepers sweeping their stoops, or to follow the steep narrow lanes uphill or down, follow the turns and sharp angles, the whole place maze-like but without mystery, except perhaps whether the spot of sunlight where one finds the black cat will be more a white square or a yellow rhombus on the cobbles at this hour? That is, if the cat is there.

ANOTHER WORLD AFLOAT ON FIRE

They swam that summer in the quarry pits filled in with years of rain. After work (summer jobs) until stars—strung up— turned on one at a time, they'd dive into the mineral-thick water, taste the abandoned and the mined at the silt-clotted depths, taste the tang of their bloods' own iron, it seemed, when they broke the surface for air. Some nights the lights of the city, a dome off in the humid air, seemed another world, another world afloat on fire. He was a scholar of nothing but the body: slack after love, freighted with whiskey, a fist of pain in his back having loaded semis that day with fireworks. Or freefalling in a dream only to wake with a start to another day of work with which he afforded the evening and another night with her.

A LARGE EXPANSE OF GLASS SET UPON TWIN SAWHORSES

At the art opening, you move from room to room, through galleries of dust intricately arranged, read the little curatorial cards the size and height of a light switch. Thin smoke insinuates from a snuffed wick.

You, you say to yourself (startled, having assumed you were alone as you watched dust breed on a large expanse of glass set upon twin sawhorses) as you find your own reflection marooned there.

THE LONELINESS OF A BRIDGE

The bridge, a field of tensions, holds up the weight of the moon. The bridge scrapes the accretions back, finds a shape left by the body: a cusp, a threshold. As if to hush the history of the bridge, shadows suggest a solidity elsewhere. The bridge is a camouflage's erasure, a mirror's transience. After a morning of access errors, the bridge fails to heed the portents, to strike an economy of means. As apparent contradictions reconcile, the bridge cannot shake a vague feeling. The bridge teeters on an imperfect grid. The bridge is an invention called *the bridge*. The bridge is impervious to modifications, structured as it is to accommodate the passing hours of a chronic illness. The bridge holds a temple's midday darkness. The story of the bridge unfolds as if a map, and like a map, is hard to fold back after use.

THE WEIGHT

I pulled into Nazareth, was feelin' about half past dead
—The Band

He does not notice its dead, leaden weight until he has time on his hands. A single second is heavier than a sack of flour. He would need a car jack to budge a half an hour an inch off the floor. At night in bed, he cannot breathe. The hours stack up one by one like stones upon his chest.

SOME WILL TELL YOU THEIR SECRET

Some will tell you the world is all there is: the chameleon and the chamomile, the shadbush and the shaddock. Some will tell you the soul is a flame, and you will wonder which flame: the flash catching up to the struck match? The constancy of the stove's pilot light? Or a prairie fire skittering across the acres? Others will say that all you see is a lie, that the bees balanced on the oregano, the raspberries full ripe in pungent shade, and the baby calmed by a simple carol, are but the shadowed half-truth of a fallen realm. What you see, they'll say, is a fabrication, a knotted cloth by which you are blindfolded. They will lift the hurricane lamp's charred globe and let the glass fall and shatter. Some will tell you the things of this world are inspired, and that a single breath shaped that glass globe, and unseen, shapes all. Some will tell you nothing and pretend they hold a secret. Some will tell you their secret just to watch it spread like a virus.

YET THE PAST HARDLY EXISTED

Adam did not name the animals, but remembered their names, one by one as each approached. Sometimes he thought he had forgotten, but the name was right there on the tip of his tongue. Even the phrase *the tip of my tongue* existed before he could speak it, as did all words: *sugar, engram,* and *ebb*. His own fluency—*thin clouds above the cove, quarry edge, crow on a prayer wheel, linden pollen*—left him off-kilter, a bit seasick with a continual sense of *déjà vu*. Each word he recalled seemed a premonition, and yet the past hardly existed. *Last night* or *day-before-yesterday* he could name, but never recollect.

GATES SWUNG OPEN ONE AFTER ANOTHER TO ADMIT US

in memory of Marvin Bell

We went north and not without difficulty as we fled the rebels. When the hills were white with moon, we left. We traveled the long distance on foot and whenever we begged from strangers along the road we felt shame. Here and there sparrows called in the ravines. We met no one returning from the opposite direction. I held my daughter close to my chest, feared her cry might bring wolves or tigers. She squirmed and cried louder.

Thunderstorms darkened half of the ten days we traveled. Struggling to make our way through mud—the eroded paths slippery—we held on hand to hand. Our clothes were black with rain. After such difficulties one day, we covered only a couple of miles. Mornings we waded through cold water among stream-smoothed stones; evenings, we rested at the sky's ledge beneath mountain mist. Low pine branches provided little shelter and we ate what wild berries we could find. At last, we made a short pause in our journey near a marsh before we continued.

A dear friend lived just below the pass—there his kindness reached beyond the gathering clouds. We arrived as dusk gave way to darkness. Gates swung open, one after another, to admit us. Heated water was brought, and we bathed our feet. Around us servants lit lamps. Strips of paper were cut and hung to recall our wandering souls. His wife and children greeted us and seeing our condition, cried. My poor children had to be >

roused when platters of food were carried into the hall.

We should swear always to be like brothers! My friend said. Rooms were prepared for us and we felt at home. In uncertain times, how have I found such trust? A year has passed since we separated. Still the rebels fight in the south. How I wish I had a heron's wings that I might fly at once to be with you, my friend, again.

AN ECHO & ITS GLYPH

Slope determines the seep, as logic coheres despite the slippages.

The subjects of poetry elude words. Form threatens the space it occupies. At summer's end, summer ends. In the way that a poem is a torn parcel, or a nest of twine, or an echo and its glyph, the future is merely a placeholder. The dreamer awake will lose grasp of the dream as it unwinds like a nightgown from a drowned woman's face.

The curtains will rustle between acts with the gerundive stillness of arrival.

SHELTER IN PLACE

A square roofed with a triangle as you drew it as a child. Windows blank. The water trickles down only to stagnate. Floorboards warp. Wallpaper sags. Black moss velvets the banister. Swallows dart from chimney chinks. Call it the spirit house. The house of spirits, this faded blue tarpaulin as a makeshift lean-to. This house with an echo as a tenant. This house dark after the curfew. This requisitioned house, occupied by occupiers. This house in the magnolia's impermeable shade. This house where you grew up. Curtains drawn, a sliver of light slanting through by which to read the red-lettered words of the Savior. This house of the Lord forever, where monarchs preside over joe-pye weed. This straw house. This stick house where you can hide, sieve out the arbitrary from the dream, grow indifferent to questions of belief.

A PARABLE

Jesus says to the crowd, "Consider the crow." The parable ends there.

WAYLAID AGAIN

Pinned to a slack, empty clothesline: a torn pale sheet of mulberry paper. On the paper: a note in an elaborate script, a calligraphy that uncoils—loose, limber—as lazily as a snake on a cold summer morning. I squint but cannot make out a word, waylaid again, stalled as always at the denouement. I long for the intimacy of an alcove—shadowed, nest-like—but emerge from a cluttered shed of webs and wasps to night tinctured with gray (not black), with the leaden absence of happenstance.

ANIMULA

Caught up in a kind of shark's purse, the animula—an inimitable glare distilled from whiteness, a brilliant flurry—attempts to slip its bounds, to *unbody* itself. How to keep the book sealed, the fascicle sewn tight while within the little soul sings (at an almost inaudible angelic frequency) her own *Song of Songs?*

THE SPECTRUM'S VIOLET END

How little is required to obtain an illusion: minor adjustments to steer attention. You look through light, dust, and air—a plasma of sorts—to see the *thing-seen,* and yet the ragged edge of digital debris will not resolve.

Like an echo repeated on a loop, it quivers and oscillates: a thread snagged from a dream. A sense of trickery permeates.

You are plagued by the persistent recurrence of a visual image after the stimulus has been removed. The most common healing practice is touch.

Nevertheless, you are left thumb-worn as each moment is restaged with disquieting accuracy and an entire spectrum must be once again intuited from a black and white snapshot. You live here outside the mercurial borders without which there would be no trespass, nothing to forgive. Entangled in the everyday, you take down the strip of caution tape from the doorframe and enter again a place transformed. You do not and will not address the hypothetical.

Your mind is elsewhere: the painted background of mis-en-scene, an ever-widening range of countless grays and blacks on a fiberboard substrate. You keep forgetting the subgenre of the cumulative tale, the myth of specific gravity.

Roots upheave a concrete slab. Forms recur indifferently in the archival footage of the hinterlands.

As frequently as the wind, the magnetic poles switch orientation. Did you believe somehow that a sensation could be consistent *and* sustainable, could be recollected *and* reassembled, experienced again, not as a rhyme of the previous sensation but as the clone of the first sensation, its same self?

The flood, illuminated by the floodlight, looks like a wide plain of needle ice, a ragged passage over a thousand broken magic lantern slides. You are on another mistaken quest for God, ill equipped and ill at ease with the immediacy of the present tense.

You spend all night in the library bent over the card catalog. A few grains of discernible light adrift in the foyer. A transistor radio in the stacks, volume low, tuned to 1971.

You have forgotten the astrolabe's function, have abandoned the grid, the increments, and units of measurement, the offered and opened hand, the breadth and length, even, of the here and now. The past darkens like fog-murk toward the spectrum's violet end. Cloaked in a drab camouflage that neither hides nor mimics—tomorrow stalls ahead. All the clocks have stopped. How to recalibrate the gears, to recalculate the pendulum's weight and arc?

ON THE FULCRUM OF *OF*

A disorder of acute angles; memory of an interior; eight views of a river; a bird's nest of *kanji;* the mark of an interaction; the last remnants of an undisclosed substance; the transit of memory; a mode of understanding outside normal experience; a thread instead of welds; the gravity, the pull of the *not-known;* the labor of classification; the seasonal shift of light; the luminosity of deep water lit from beneath; an unlimited field of differentials; a fringe of swampland; the invisibility of things hidden in plain sight; the objectivity of the recording; the fatigue of being; the haunt of meaning; the ornament of grammar; the clench of a fig; the crook of the creek; one of nine planets demoted; prior to the invention of the sacraments; "Is not," Barthes asks, "the most erotic portion of a body *where the garment gapes*?"; the ashen residue of straw; the tangle of whispers; the banked ember of a secret; a clot of orchids; a pavilion of honey; cocoon of exhaustion; through the lens of a needle's eye; to walk across the shards of words toward meaning; nothing, of course, balances out in the end.

I'M GONNA RUN TO THE CITY OF REFUGE

A Tomb for Blind Willie Johnson

The snare impedes passage. I have an incorrigible faith. I have irrevocable desires. Each a shift from the norm. A deviation. There are moments when I am no longer in flight nor perched. In the desert, a little hummock of unprocessed uranium. Within the circle of an offramp, a coppice crazed with kudzu. On the dashboard, an outdated map of the arctic. I say to myself often in dreams, "It's just a matter of time." But what *is* the matter of time? How do I measure the increments of *just enough* or, in kin with others, unweave the sacred code? Once, I looked up from beneath the warm delta water and beheld the limp tail and dangling limbs of a gator afloat. Then the rain lifted. Is an image captivating because it is captured? I was present but forgot to present the presentation. I was obscured, if not slightly hidden. The angels were there. I was without refuge or the concealment of a trap. I was standing in the need of prayer.

ARIA

To fall asleep, I replay as a loop in my head the three minutes and four seconds of Glenn Gould's 1981 recording of the Aria from the Goldberg Variations. A flexed and continuous line.

In my dream: distant bell fragments fragrant with echoes. I sit still on a train. The landscape moves. Smoke blooms from my father's mouth. At the frozen lake's center, my mother's hand is tense on a rudder. Or is it the cold that makes her shake so?

The 1955 recording is one minute and fifty-two seconds—the melody rushes like the view out a train window, a strobe of tunnel lights amplifying the headlong pace.

Gould died of a stroke a year after the 1981 recording, as would my father a year after that.

The variations, I learned today, were composed for a patron besieged by insomnia, to be played by one of Bach's students, Goldberg, to ease the patron to sleep.

My mother's hand is on the rudder, but the boat encased in ice does not budge.

TRUST-BUILDING EXERCISE

It wasn't our story to tell, one of us argued, so we didn't. Only one of us knew the conversation was being recorded. We remembered enough to know we were beginning to forget. Each of us would have started the story at a different point. Did we have whole dreams and remember only parts? Or were the dreams themselves partial? Memories were like islands in an archipelago. Such a distance to return to them, one of us insisted. We had only the best intention. We could not agree: was it *depend, deepened,* or *deep end*? Only one of us had the home team advantage. The one we called *the magician* was in fact a juggler. Irony forgives a little at least, we agreed, the sting is not as searing as satire. As an exercise in trust, we set out to graph a murmuration of starlings in real time.

BORDER CROSSING

The conspiracy theory spreads. The same old same old: spectral figures in a liminal space, the characteristic vacancy of a vacant lot. Wind turns the weathercock. There, on the cusp of logic, we call the crows with a clap and chart chance. Horses cross from the island at low tide. A cloud where the island should be. A whole cloud in a tide pool. Falling flowers hide the figure of Krishna. We brought the wrong map but follow it, nevertheless. Brought along the wheel, the lever, and the screw. At the border, the customs official is hungry for English conversation, but speaks only in incomplete sentences:

A cornfield north of Clear Lake, Iowa

A ruckus in the rookery

Chet Baker singing "My Funny Valentine"

How disappointing, we concurred, upon finally hearing it, is the nightingale's song.

A PRE-EXISTING CONDITION

The resident alien wakes tremulously, reports to the courthouse.

The resident alien practices disorientation, keeps journals, keeps house.

The resident alien builds a passageway of latticed panels.

The resident alien draws a blank.

The resident alien helps the crepe myrtle shed its bark.

In the still photograph, how can one tell if the resident alien is landing or taking off, in motion or merely posing?

Seventy percent of those surveyed find the resident alien *unruly*.

The resident alien refuses to carry placards or banners, to join in any chants.

Grunge, the resident alien argues, describes better the costume of the performers than the music itself.

Ensnared by surveillance, the resident alien has a pre-existing condition.

Like most people, the resident alien has little time for poetry, what passes for poetry.

The resident alien has not always been a resident alien.

The resident alien's nom de plume is *the resident alien*.

As the credits run and the houselights come on, the resident alien waits for others to exit the theater first.

HEARING VOICES

The voice-over, calm, evenly paced, is meant to soothe. At any moment, one is told, machines will become sentient. One stands in the camera frame as in a trap: stuck. The spaces one occupies are transitional, peripheral: corridors, stairs, gates, a balcony that steps off into fog. It is neither unease nor disquiet one feels, but something on that continuum, that spectrum. Caught as one is in an odd moment, one waits without expectation, as if exempt from history. Where to locate oneself in one's estrangement? Between cohesion and fragmentation? One possesses a studied neutrality: a mute gray like grainy celluloid, flint, or old hawthorn stems. Like a nuthatch's back. The lake surface, all scrawls and divots, is rain-inscribed, overcast, violet-tinged. The magnolia, all at once in bloom, dissolves beneath the thunderstorm. As if to reassure, the voice-over speaks again with a pickpocket's intimate nearness.

THE REMAINDER

The poem's longing is for something *before* rhetoric. The given, marked by traces of use, is undone, as if one, bewildered by enigma, might raise the dead or draw down the moon, out of phase at midsummer.

A bonfire transforms into a reindeer and outruns an arrow in flight.

What does one do with the remainder? The discarded? The pinch of salt that cannot balance the scales? *If only*. If only one could be reduced to tears.

REPEAT-TO-FADE

in memory of Larry Levis

I want to begin again as mineral. Or perhaps a horse. One could do worse than a horse. A glut of fallen persimmons rots on the path. Milkweed silk floats by. I'll begin again as mineral deep in autumn's dark harbor. Or be a horse with the irrational mind of a slumbering saint. It could be worse. Illness might make me a stranger to myself and those I love. The abject lurks. The songs don't *end* but repeat-to-fade. Beech leaves will hold on—yellowed, papery—all winter. When my heart feels heavy, I often think of Larry, his sudden exit. In my dream, a gurney blocks his doorway. The EMTs can't get around it.

Larry would have returned as a horse if he could. But, as Lorca writes, *what an effort!*

THE FUTURE PERFECT: A FUGUE

How does memory slip through the viscosity of time? How does a subfloor support the weight of trauma, an archive of dreams, a cast iron tub overflowing? With a retrospective glance, one can see clearly the narrative's broken sequence—mute bodies in motion, staggered by desire, more a dance than drama. In the scrubbed-out distance, a magpie, old emblem of confusion, calls out workbook phrases it learned in captivity: a seductive hubbub, a sweet and oracular chatter.

: :

Calling it a *blue distilled from dusk* does not change the fact that a shadow has no tangible content.

: :

Wherever one walks, a cloud of gnats hovers head-high. Starlings break fast from a pear tree. Twilight lingers long above the tree line. A deer and fawn bed down beneath dark hemlocks. As the future approaches, a chained dog begins to whimper.

: :

From an excavated meteorite, hauled up on the shingled shore, a single frequency emanates. Distance defies clarity and cannot be fixed. It withdraws. No. It encroaches. There's just enough light to reveal the dark interior of the icebergs gathered out there like the clustered notes of a chord.

>

: :

How few stars to suggest the infinite?

: :

The mountain, upheaved in an instant, erodes slowly. One watches the mountain move, watches the earth occlude the moon. Cold holds down clouds just above the tree line. The coyote's movements are tracked and mapped. Now and then a loss of signal or glitch registers as a vanishing.

: :

As a giant in Eden, one is given the ornaments of grammar, the ornaments of wilderness. Beneath a hunter's moon, one shelters in the cave of allegory. Back then, by which one means *now,* everything was in the public domain: zero, for instance, and the golden ratio. One is given the whiteness of salt, the whiteness that is sky. Is it *disillusion* or *dissolution* one experiences first?

: :

What one said returned echoed: the fog stood still; the mountain moved.

: :

Several days into the journey, lured by the horizon's curve (and to enliven the plot), one emerges as a stowaway. At what depth will the light not penetrate? Bewitched, the compass needle points its one direction.

: :

In the wake of marks and traces, how to itemize the pandemonium? How to accommodate the allusion without a source—the washed-out silk of mirage, the wash on the line—and not botch the figures and sums? To say *gesture* is to evoke a body involved in the making. Has the dance begun before the dancers move?

: :

Sometimes one's convinced one's seen a ghost. One feels faint and for a moment vision blurs. A bit of gold leaf snagged on an acacia shimmers at a high frequency in the breeze. Such quickened enthusiasms! Such transport! The dizzying quiver and flux soon pass. The search is never for fire—all motion and efficiency—but for a contraption impregnated by light.

: :

What matters is the miscellany, the hodgepodge, the mishmash, unkempt days loosely stitched to the next, a hinge giving in to rust, to the slow passage of rust, or the mind at its usual unruly industry, as noisy as gravel in a zinc bucket, a medley, a potpourri, a salmagundi, the moon mistaken for a blossom in a mistaken translation of a Chinese poem, the mélange, the welter, the motley muddle, the train as it approaches the station trailing smoke—an amalgam of combustible cinders, an alloy of smudge and ash. One could lose sleep making sense of the grab bag of all the *this* and the *that,* the hash, the rehash, the leftovers, the gumbo a different recipe in each spoonful. Like it or not, the sundries accumulate: a collection without taxonomy, a torn crazy quilt, a ragbag of hand-me-downs.

: :

On the garden's raised beds, the moon is a white scab of salt. If only experience were immediate, which is to say, >

unmediated. A single slug scales a cabbage stalk. In the distance: an inscrutable verge, so far away it remains to be seen.

: :

Stone tools outlive their usefulness. Voids and solids, reconfigured, are called a room, a house, an interior. Memories gather there as residue, as dust. Duration suggests a beginning and end, yet there is no recollection of birth or death. For now: these notes, these intervals.

: :

Beyond: blunted peaks, cloud-girdled. The air rare, white as limestone, vivid. Two trees endure in the old orchard. Like a contraption in a disappearing act, a cloth-covered birdcage hangs by a wire. Appearances, noted in the present, occur as all things light-revealed, lit by the past.

: :

The sky and sea are drab, grainy: a long passage of sleep without dreams, without underpinnings or a lacework of roots. Does one affix the memory of tides to some tidal memory, without a middle distance to distinguish the *near* from the *far,* the idea of *north* from *true north* itself?

: :

From Europa's cracked crust, icy plumes vent. Worlds, unlimited, come into being and perish. While planting an olive tree, a treasure is uncovered. Salt is angular, twisted; bitter is unsymmetrical, smooth. Amber attracts chaff as a lodestone draws iron fillings. Is stasis or motion a proper attribute of the soul? Iron is, consequently, hard. And lead is heavy.

: :

The sky—taut, silken—is stripped back with turpentine, blurred by time. The path is a scar. Each mark conceals a belabored query. A barricade of tires burns at the border. Slung rocks plummet like sudden hail.

: :

How not to project into the future, not to see the past as portent? Light exposes the image. Exposed to light, the image begins to disintegrate.

: :

The owls are not oracles, or the sparrows a scintilla of God's attention. Each room in the apiary is hexagonal, overfull with viscous ooze. How soon before the last colony collapses?

: :

One arrives with an invitation of ether and stars. One arrives exhausted. One arrives to a fanfare, to the erasures of amnesia. One arrives with a pre-existing condition, although the symptoms mask themselves. In the grip of pleasure, one arrives. What of the narrative can a single frame hold? A closed door? As always, the concurrent must be conveyed in sequence. A door opens onto a frayed fog-edge, onto an eroded boundary, onto a shadow-cast of lilacs. The past, scuttled, is still visible beneath the surface. Look: a pool of glacial melt, light from the north, the dusk's blue palette. By recognizing objects in photographs one proves again one is not a robot.

: :

>

What is that bush called swamped in purple blossoms, a ragged notation gone wild, at once threshold and passage? In rough wind, it's a pentimento of reconsidered brushstrokes.

: :

Between figure and ground, a stage is set for the viewer. The parallel plots, being parallel, never waver or intersect. And watching, reckoning with time, one feels not exiled but displaced, surrounded by the dredged-up and extraneous, fodder and ciphers. One attempts to forget the others seated beside, behind, or in front, to forget the common experience of the darkened theater, the individual threads woven to make up the snow-blind blank space of the screen. Up close, one notices more and more subatomic particles fill in the void: blips and specks, a blurred dirty white tundra. Soon one forgets one is reading the subtitles as they appear, seven to nine syllables at a time, and one is fluent in Greek or Hungarian, or some indigenous and endangered language about to slip from usage. As an actor speaks one feels one's own tongue touch the back of one's front teeth, one's mouth opens around the air of a vowel. An *o*, perhaps. It is as though one has awakened in the night of a sleeping car to a single word spoken out of a dream clearly, directly. And in that a word: a thousand miles crossed one tie after another, the gravel bed's angle of repose shimmered, shuddered. At last undermined.

: :

Beneath the thin overlay of time, one can observe the infinite distances between two adjacent points, the slow growth of spores, the stalactite's irregular drip, even minute particles of pigment diffuse in a wash of mineral spirits.

: :

The angel—a lens in images of the Annunciation—focuses to a pinpoint the projection, but leaves no mark, no record of *having-been-there.*

: :

The past carded and spun makes a coarse thread good for rough stitches. Or tying up tomato vines. One has a ladder, but nothing to lean it against. One skirts the issue; one glimpses a slip. Boredom is a given in purgatory, as it is here.

: :

The story gets the better of the teller. Incongruous memories surface: unwilled, untitled. The obscure synopsis should have clued one in. One renames one's doubts *ambivalence.*

: :

One cuts open a hailstone and finds a crystal lattice, a bit of grit. One looks in vain for the imperfect stitch that confirms at last *handmadeness.*

: :

A truce is always fragile, as when the board of directors questions the lasting value and aesthetic merit of the recent acquisitions. One's deliberate delays do not counter impermanence, do not make visible that which otherwise remains hidden.

>

: :

In an old field recording of a chain gang's work song, the sledgehammers come down not quite in unison. The gang keeps time as well as it can be kept.

: :

Smoke enters the room, and one crawls to the fire assembly point, is accounted for, remains a safe distance from the building. One is drawn to symmetry and at home in melancholia. One cannot hear the river's sidewinding, cannot hear the rain's white noise above the fire's racket.

: :

One complains about the weight and burden of the mask, but, in fact, the mask is made of a fine silk lace and stitched rags of wasp paper. One walks face-first into a spider's web. When a snare slips, one is entangled in a bower-bird's lair, in a prickly rose.

: :

Beyond the window, intervals of blue in the middle distance lend substance to light, light to substance. In the interior space—infiltrated, light-suffused—the apparition of the body itself practices presence, the improbable possibilities of visibility.

: :

Cigarette smoke enters from off-screen. In the previous scene, someone enters the sanctum of the woods and is forbidden to gather fallen branches from the forest floor, to build a fire. The fallen snow seems a plaster cast of another, forgotten world. On the soundtrack, the pricks and glimmers of bell tones. A slow, childlike tune plucked on a cello.

: :

One could foresee the potential calamity ahead on the unfinished dance floor, but for some reason one held one's tongue and, as one anticipated, the bodies tumbled and eventually, amid the screams, the music stopped. One is encouraged to shelter in place, to make do, to hold tight. One predicts the predicament but is encouraged again to not rush into anything.

: :

The template allows one to draw every imaginable floor plan that might be pieced together from the modular units, but none seems habitable: a space one might experience as a *duration*. The stock photos hung on the wall do not help, nor the books arranged by jacket cover color, moving from cool blues to the warmest reds. One signs the lease, nonetheless. Moves in.

: :

One enters the quarantine of sleep willfully, sketches in night with a charred willow branch, with a pigment of burnt bone. One sets a trap for the moon, stretches out a parachute to collect condensation. Night eschews a chronological ordering, thus one is truant within the moment. Not *constellation,* one thinks, but *asterism.* Not a *fetish* but a *tomato-shaped pincushion.*

: :

Hourly, the pathway reconfigures itself. The Minotaur's choices seem few: right, left, straight ahead, or backtrack. The labyrinth is an architecture of elaborate and abstruse

>

logic. Logic does not comfort, but confines. If the Minotaur charges and gores a wall, the wall repairs itself. He is not cursed, but is, if truth be told, too dull-headed to learn that with a reasoned thought or two the maze will unfold itself before him into the shortest distance between two points; that he needs only to lift the heavy bull mask from his human face to find an exit sign.

: :

Ice reflects an opaque sky. As it moves through a stand of firs, the wind slips up and down its octave. Clouds scud. The day moon remains—an abrasion on glass, a nail-scratched locket, a coin defaced, a glacial basin burnished onto the firmament. Navigable inland waterways freeze. Birds fall from flight. Great swathes of forests are felled. Crops fail. Famine. Bodies unburied breed plagues and poxes. How does one avoid thinking about the *void?* One burns witches, who manipulate and control the weather; one spends what precious fuel is left.

: :

One is as restless as one who approaches an ending; as calm as one can be the quiet moment before a soliloquy begins. A sudden instant of hailstones clatters in a boat's hull. A broken stoneware jar hangs in a tree for a bird to nest in.

: :

In the attic, haunted by a single wasp, the turban fan cannot disperse the heat joists, insulation, and plywood frame in. The stacked boxes—old photos and tax files, wait as kindling for the serenade of a spark. The combustion is spontaneous; fire gives birth to fire. One stands, unscathed, at a distance from the house, and beholds the fire, the garish spectacle of its robes. The house rages but is not consumed. Ablaze, it stands as square and certain as a child's drawing of a house. In each window: flames instead of curtains.

::

A king awaits a cargo of gold, ivory, pearls, and sandalwood from Ophir. Before the treasure arrives a forest reclaims the palace. The forest is a garden: intimately scaled, adherent to a sacred geometry. Rejoice. As the seeker advances, God recedes. This is the origin of dance.

::

Along the prairie flyway, what kerning and leading holds the flock together? Each bird apart?

::

The confluence of the rivers is set down as a calligraphic abstraction. A dark reservoir without reflection, the floodplain stretches to the horizon. Which is more—*as little as possible?* Or *as much as is necessary?* Or is the question: *which is less?*

::

Winter ends with a miscellany's logic: a leaden horizon, a narrow but unbridgeable distance. Stolen moments are exchanged for isolated hours, elaborate entanglements, a lodging. One's suitable room fulfills a double assignment as a stage and shelter. The heady pollen of stargazer lilies covers the bureaus, the desktop, and end tables. Beyond the window, the sacred mountain is depleted of snow. On a frequency at the far end of the dial, one can hear >

Vespers, and recalls the little Latin one learned long ago, knowing even then it would come in handy.

: :

Thomas the Doubter enters the wound as one might a cave. To exit, as from a womb, is the difficult part.

: :

One wants not just efficiency, but a simple design as well, the way an old ballad stores an exact dose of sadness, the way a bloom of jellyfish disappears into the murk. Each problem solved, dissolves. By all accounts a hedgerow absorbs the traffic noise. How many seasons has the ladder leaned against the gutter? Far north and further afield, one kneels like a pilgrim. The canvas, roughly stitched together, keeps the sleet out. One adjusts the perpetual motion machine's flywheel between a pair of heavy magnets. Set in motion, the contraption keeps going, and because it keeps going one figures it will continue.

: :

Memory is after all a mode of abstraction, a navigational marker anchored in endlessness. Given the state one's in, one just might carry a candlestick across a distance to illuminate not the *invisible,* but the *unviable.* What is the provenance of that skull at the foot of the cross? Why does one find oneself so often a fixture in a disquieting tableaux?

: :

A mirror cannot affix the fleeting, cannot conjoin temporalities in complex narratives. Although one stands ruthlessly naked before it, the mirror sees as if for the first time. Assisted by another mirror, a mirror performs the trick of infinite repetition, constructs a corridor of receding echoes. Call it an *image apparatus* or *looking glass,* its only art is mimicry.

: :

Today is a series of small interventions—neither fugue, nor aftermath—a hedge, perhaps, against some future loss. The ordinary is preordained, even as a slight shift in scale emerges preserved in the *now.* The room itself, a façade, before which a drama unfolded, is scrubbed of context, of isolated gestures, as if, having never seen the movie, one recalled an isolated film still, the way shadow fell so that no single face is illuminated. Whatever *has been* or is *about to be* is lit poorly. Nonetheless, one has moved on, even as the empire declines into ruin, and the bones of giants are exhumed. *Nonetheless,* one says, getting little traction.

: :

To resolve the apparent discord of two notes in an empty room with piano, a third note is sounded. Longing pervades. One understands this, as one understands the frail luster of afternoon light on a plum—neither red nor purple—but oddly buttery. How to narrate desire as more than ache? As less than narrative? After the first two, the third note slips from hearing.

: :

A photograph of a windswept arctic expanse entitled *A Sublime & Icy Prospect.* A coat stitched from nettles. The sensation of a tongue pressed against a loosened tooth. Wax cylinder recordings of soliloquies. Scrap silver. A peripheral drift. The reservoir of a notebook. The archive >

as a point of departure. A Florentine window above Santo Spirito. An instance of clairvoyance dismissed.

: :

A retinue of sleepwalkers gains the other shore. Soon they will open doors, which open onto doors, which open onto doors. One waits on the other side: one's passport still in the custom agent's hand, still under the custom agent's scrutiny, unstamped.

: :

Overnight, a circle of mushrooms appears: black-gilled, their caps pocked, frog-belly white, their annuli torn—ragged foreskins—abominable, obscene, ill-omened.

: :

A note from a flute of elder wood. A fabricated diary. The water a boat displaces. The future as a place of exile. The photograph as a caesura between *before* and *after.* The grid and its austere function. The *m* that distinguishes a *comma* from a *coma*. Alluvial marshlands. The borrowing of one's enemy's arrows. The object rehabilitated through reuse. Incidental objects on a minor planet. A dark chamber fitted with a lens. An exemplar liberated from rebirth. The murmur of ink drying.

: :

On either side of the street, the dogs long ago settled their territorial dispute. No one dances these days upon the worn floorboards of the union hall. Next door a young woman fastens a necklace of seed pearls, recalls the fragile wingspan of her mother's collarbones. From a throng of sleet, the caretaker emerges and jiggles a wrong key in the lock. When one dog barks, the other starts as per the conditions of their treaty.

: :

The soul, seeking sweetness, departs the body as a bee, delineates from the chaos a path among black-eyed Susans, alighting here and there on the surface tension of time, teetering as wind intervenes in the grasses and treetops. A memory reiterated becomes a *new,* an *other* memory, and whatever has been accentuated or occluded is no less real. The subject, of course, is the simultaneity of *what happened,* the narrative inferred by what the eavesdropper misheard, the elisions and incongruities smoothed out, but the clutter undistilled. It is not surprising the attention the barely discernable receives, the gaps and exclusions in the pulse of rain, for instance, or the erasures, which, upon a second look, are quite evident. The soul—there must be a rational explanation—comes and goes at will, possesses a lucid and somber solidity. Today: a bee. Tomorrow: a lizard or perhaps a little armored pill bug, (the only crustacean, by the way, fully adapted to life on land). It is essential to narrows one's subject, but the digressions pile up like loess, shift and collapse as one attempts to walk away.

: :

The screen flares then settles into its grayish white. The film, snapped, clacks against the reel.

: :

One stands at last in front of the house the locals call *The House of the Hanged Man.* Having come a long way, one senses beyond the treeline some force or foreboding. There is no record of the hanged man or of a hanging in the town archives. No doubt there is an explanation. One >

enters without knocking, as is the custom, and calls out. No one answers. Ravels of threads stand in as curtains. A toppled ladder-back chair occupies the dining room, but no rope hangs from the exposed rafters, which slump beneath the roof's ongoing collapse. A little rain (it's started to rain since one entered) falls on the stone floor. From the unshuttered windows, one takes in the upward slope, the restrained palette of the medieval hilltop town. Is it possible to enter uninvited and remain politely distant? So as not to be provocative, thunder waits until one has forgotten the presence of lightning to sound, and the rain, like a clock, ticks on the stone casements. In the valley, perhaps, wolves disrupt the foxhunt. The mown hay molders in the fields. The day, just about to pivot to evening, shines like a polished stone, something one might pick up on a path and pocket, only to find later while doing the wash and wonder why this stone and not another? One sets the stone upon a sill, nonetheless: a keepsake kept after all, like the name of this house for its namesake.

: :

Not the gloaming or the interface of first light, but the point in one's movement called *here.*

: :

Jesus, the wounded healer, descends a dark, steep stairwell to the realm of the dead. Sometimes night comes, but the edges don't meet. Sometimes it's dark enough to see stars. Jesus has yet to learn patience, the theological difference between *both* and *either/or.* A precarious light, he holds up a vast distance crossed. A linga of flame, he flares but nothing catches. The dead, by reflex, turn away from his scalded flesh.

: :

A flame's pneumatic body. The charred spent tip of a match. A house without mirrors. Multiple readings of the empty space. To say *There is nothing I want. Nothing at all.* An arrested motion. An apnea. The drama of scale. The surface pearlescent. The currents awry. An exhumed ship's hull marl-blackened, skeletal. A world sung into being. The equity of light and shadow. To say *I wanted for nothing, but wanted nonetheless.*

: :

The story so far is all rehearsal, what one calls *standard procedure,* and no date set for the performance. To add edge to uncertainty, the problem is a problem of vigilance and one is down to a skeleton crew. One admits one is an emptied skiff, a placeholder, a null field. To recognize the invisible, one approximates the infinite. It's total immersion or nothing.

: :

Far fewer days ahead than behind. And each set down in parallel graphite lines. Although ruled, errors and random interference interrupt the parallel; give the graph the look of lake water after a breeze has passed, of ripples diminishing at an almost steady rate. One recalls now one almost drowned in this lake in 1966. Above: clouds cut from jade. Clouds uprooted.

: :

Fog is the weft; fog is the warp: a weave without visible increments. The boat's wake arrives before the boat. The argument is tangled, tangential. A spun thread is drawn long, the curve of its slack calculable. In a Venetian >

ambrotype, the dome's oculus returns God's gaze.

: :

One longs to align the elements, to disrupt invisibility, but only the ancillary emerges in moonlight. The hills and mesas inscribed by rain and wind are like scrolls and codices. How vast forgetting becomes. One looks up and finds a momentary map of meteors, a thread not yet entirely severed. One turns to cosmology, numerology, mysticism, and analysis to disinter the past, when a shovel would do the trick. Wind's tremolo through cottonwoods documents distance. The moon, held down by a jagged line of solder, does not set. What can be unearthed by way of a long exposure? One lives in the rain shadow. An unkempt edge delineates the property line: a little wilderness to keep others out. One is guilty often of the trespass of a gaze, yet whatever is seen is partial: a diffuse reflection in an isolated body of water, for instance. How does one, as Willa Cather suggests, *imprison for a moment the shining?* The first intent was to catch fire, then to release it.

: :

What if one spoke only in the future perfect? What if, as it leapt, the tiger atomized into a swarm of bees? What if the day-before-yesterday did not hover in the blind spot, a schism between abstraction and figuration? What if one refused to watch the effigies torn apart, re-sewn, and torn apart again?

SELF-CARE

As if to forestall the fall of night, they move into a house furnished with the previous owner's possessions. A much-handled pear remains unripe in a basket on the table: a dream nested within another dream. It is hard to imagine that the gray meteorites, set upon the mantel as keepsakes, each the size of a chickadee's egg, once glowed: a blaze across the sky. The previous owner's books are burned, not for their content, but for the heat released. Between the drawn bowstring and the arrow's notch: a gap of time. They do not burn the booklet from the HMO, but leave it open to the chapter called "When and When Not to Call the Doctor," which offers instructions, with illustrations, on how to remove a fishhook from one's own eye.

OBLIQUE STRATEGIES

A motionless nimbus, isolated from the cloud-cluster, suspends above my head. Whatever happens before a camera is a performance: Jupiter dwarfed by the moon, for instance, or the door not ajar but lifted off its hinges. The crows gyre up all at once. As vulnerable as one is in a trance, I am caught in the wake of my own displacement. I find as a workaround a shallow flight of stairs, a vignette (*as from a vine*). Like a sleepwalker, I wait for the reverb, for the waves to break their silence.

THE SICK BOY

The child is about to wake or about to give into sleep. The time of sickness passes like a dense current of fog that moves around him as he stands still or parts uneasily as he steps into and through it. The fog is like a snowstorm, a whiteout, but not cold. Moments of clarity break through. What to call them—visions? He is a child which means he is not whole, complete, finished, or singular. He is fragmented, split like a dropped vial of mercury. Atomized. He is the child nonetheless the heavenly host addresses, and he hears it when others cannot distinguish it from birdcall, wind in the attic, and radio waves. If seen by someone from a distance, the child imagines he would be out of focus, a blur, a figure not wholly solid, like a ghost or cloud wisp. A near-sighted boy, that is how he see distant things—lights haloed, aflare, the edges of trees smudged against the sky, the sky grainy. Translucent. Dispersed. He wants to be well. Returned to school and the hurry of the day. At school he is known as *the sick boy*. Hand-drawn cards encourage him to *get well soon*. He has been sick for as long as he can remember. Yet what can he remember? One day a new refrigerator arrives, and he is allowed to spend the entire day inside its abandoned cardboard box, which he imagines a space station, a jail house, a bunker. But the next day it is folded up curbside with the rest of the trash. This is still years before the moon landing, the riots, the city an underlit dome of smoke in the distance. What is wrong with the child? That is what everyone is trying >

to figure out. Exploratory surgery is scheduled. They will open him and see, his mother says. In a new movie called *The Fantastic Voyage,* a miniature submarine with doctors and scientists on board enters a man's body by way of a syringe. His mother says they will open him and see. He imagines his insides out—unpacked, unraveled, fingered, scrutinized, held up to the light—only to be repacked and, if he had the word, he would hope not *haphazardly.* First, they will put him under, then open him and see.

THE HISTORY OF THE SIEGE

1

One beholds the once-familiar landscape as an arrangement: each fog-obscured hill and ravine bearing a quietude. There is no way to translate the blur into precision. Up close: dusky purples; far away a pearled gray. The distance, a trace of a tracing, is mute, remote. The grackles, unseen, helix up and away to an elsewhere, and take the whirl of their racket with them.

2

One stays tuned in, as asked, listens to the click of the reel-to-reel as it reels. For a shape-shifter, vertigo often follows the shift. The antecedent seems prescient in retrospect. Within the mob, one sheds the *self* like a tattered shirt. To the museum exhibiting its own anachronism, one brings hammers, saws, and axes. One embraces the flaws and discrepancies of the shamanic object. The dream, hand-sewn, is vague, elusive—a deliberate and overly determined encounter with an operation of chance.

3

Shadows lurk. Mistakes and alterations accumulate: a web of radio signals, an inventory of rhymes sealed in cold wax. How to begin or begin again when the unit of measure is not yet agreed upon? When all signs of sky are eliminated? Here the prescribed converges with the >

unintended: a perfume's balanced elements, an emerald flash of a starling's wing, or, perhaps, the groom's complicity. One does not wish to acquire the property or inquire about it: discarded, derelict as it is. But one inquires, acquires. One feels safe opting out of the latest manifestation of Futurism, which, fast-paced as it is, swings around again at a hurried and manic pace.

4

Beyond the grid of streets: dwellings and storage units at the sinkhole's edge, hawthorns—hung with mementos—as ad hoc monuments. As if some god descended as a cloud, hindsight is obscured. The story, at first withheld, is subverted by its feverish retelling, unsewn stitch-by-stitch, given over to entropy, uncertainty, and randomness. In the shelter of an archive, one has second thoughts about the efficacy of nostalgia, rethinks the idea of *shelter*. The signal, jammed, comes through nonetheless as its own fugue of distortion, a shivery notation on tape, a loop the length of which is unpredictable and thus alluring. There is ample time these days for precise measurements, recalculations, and the showing of one's work. The extra sheets of scratch paper add up and one keeps them in a drawer for some future project. One day's residue settles upon the next and soon is blown into corners and under sofas, gathers inbetween the floorboards. One thinks of oneself not as *displaced* but as *relocated*, and takes a certain comfort in the distinction.

5

When one writes: *the silky plumage of a crow's extended wing,* no corvid flies forth. No mulberry trees emerge from valley fog. All is quiet in the cocoonery. From here, it is hard to hear the rustle of fibers pulled long, the hot air vented. As a crystal suggests the enduring pattern of its atoms, in these words, one hopes to suggest a shape. Not a rook or magpie, not a jackdaw or jay, but a crow.

6

One had hoped to adhere to a plan of modest gestures toward some faultless whole, knowing all along that each thought was apt to be interrupted, and that one had brought a cant hook and peavey to a job where a set of tweezers and a fine-eyed needle would most likely come in handy, and thus everything took on a mottled, scrubby look, the splintery surface like a bed of sleet where one does at last fall asleep, but dreams of thorns.

7

The distance enlarges. Ditches, streams, runs, and rivers rush headlong, braid and diverge like looping forms of a floral arabesque, a baroque composition of spilled silks, toward the elsewhere of a delta, where deposited sediment settles and the waters merge, estuarial. Metaphors entwine, as in some rite of spring, and logic unsettles. In a noisy, violet twilight of catbirds, the witch hazel and the willow are again touched with green. The difficulty is always arrival. One travels but forgets the *in-between.* Summer rains replenish the aquifer. Arctic ice melts. Sea floors spread as a subducted plate slips. The >

longest day, nonetheless, feels abbreviated. The ghost never leaves the foyer. It has just arrived. It is about to depart. The plot is the usual: abduction, shipwreck, mistaken identity, and amorous confusion; otherwise known as *the process of elimination.* A spirit level brought to bear would prove the whole thing level, but level to what?

8

One surrenders and is thus rendered. One cannot unbraid the wick's sooty ends. One draws the dream of the wolves, but then remembers only the drawing and not the dream. One attributes the whispered *shush* to the crescent moon. One builds the walls solid and only later cuts out the door and windows. One kindles the fragile laurel twigs with pitch. To end the initiation (or is it *irritation*?), one admits that the Tao cannot be conveyed by either words or silences. One unties the bride's hair. One continues in a single direction that cannot be reversed. One recalls, as if it were a single hour, cedars in sleet and the damp heat beneath a revival tent. One follows an igneous river to Pluto's dusky domain. One courts discord and is shortchanged. The moment is ephemeral, yet one is always *in* it.

9

Classification and nomenclature are one's business, noting, for instance, the vernal slippage from *folks* to *fox,* the difference between *crabapple winter* and *false spring,* between the floating world and all that it displaces. A keyhole frames the beyond. Edges are lost to a hand-held lantern's unruly glares and tinted shadows that jostle as one stumbles. In one's other hand: a hazel rod like a blind man's cane. One walks the horizon's halo; at the river, crosses for a third time the devil's bridge. Each thought, embodied in flame, flares, then falls as acrid smoke.

10

One is hitchhiking on a back road. Waiting is always longer when one's task is waiting. And it is winter. Snow drifts against the wall of a ruined corncrib. The remains of dried vines seem to hold the whole thing up. The slatted wall provides little shelter from wind. Hard not to envy the dead, who travel light, and have a destination in mind, which is just up the road a spell.

11

One begins to distinguish among species of boredom, heretofore-unnoticed textures and quirks, forms of repetition, bewildering stasis: both the impasse of shame *and* the allure of a lack. Rushed, as one is in the meantime, one observes a wind-rocked lotus pod and imagines a poetics of leisure, the cadence of hours, the coincidence and discord, the wake of silence that follows. The past is not a story, but merely a map, legible only in retrospect. One had hoped to escape the obvious aspects of melancholy—distant thunder, the elaborate deceptions of a minimal disguise, the crippling effect of gravity upon a soul—but finds the ellipses stand in for far more than one might have predicted, given the evidence as well as the delay and interference in transmission.

>

12

Chased, one can plot out the pursuit curve; can hear the descending scale of wind over reeds; can behold the shimmered mirage-edge of a headlong god, as if he were merely a screen glitch, or some slapdash graffiti. A memoir is a ruin. Or is it that memory ruins? One had hoped that the chocks and wedges would hold the fractured fragments together *and* apart: the damage archived, called-attention-to. Or is it a damaged archive one foresees? One had feared an inauspicious sign—a ring of deer in a clearing, a congregation of sparrows on a guy-wire—but received instead a bill from EZ-pass for an unpaid toll on a car one donated years ago to one's local NPR station. Water subsides and one forgets the tension of surfaces, forgets the sun haze beyond the smolder.

13

One indexes the passage of time, and in doing so disrupts the ephemeral nature of shadow. Even from here the frequency emitted by the broom's worn edge can be detected. One is often of two minds, ill at ease with the initial sketch, with the associated truths and inherent deceptions. The development of cities coincides with the earliest known script, used primarily for the purpose of inventory. One is tempted to read backward into a previous text a prophecy. The fathom of an hour, seen fleeting, never comes quite into focus: *now* already forgotten by *then*. An empty bowl holds hinterland echoes. As in the endless afterlife of a diorama, ancient dragonflies hover above reed beds. The aperture allows light to enter, to be confined in a hollow box.

14

One is at the midpoint between the pole and the equator. Shade pulls one out of the sun. If only one could subtract memory, perhaps then the overlay of intuition would not be so ill-fitting, so stifling. A computer-generated weather system offers a rebus of clichés. The common denominator remains to be seen. A cloud? A lightning bolt? Should one stoke or starve the fire? No one, of course, takes the prerequisite and thus the curriculum's scope and sequence are kerflooey. An elegy is the most common of souvenirs.

15

One awaits sensitivity training. One awaits confirmation that one was switched at birth. One awaits payment for another hour of uncompensated labor. One awaits the enemy's surrender. One awaits acoustic phenomena built from megadata and algorithms to mimic random sounds. One awaits the leashed cormorant's resurfacing. One awaits an appointment's appointed hour. One awaits an invitation. One awaits the obfuscation of hierarchies. One awaits the slim glimpse of flesh in the fold of the folding screen. One awaits the resurgence of superstition, the interim between storms, between sonnets in a crown of sonnets. In the meantime, one waits.

16

One comes to expect the jump cut of a *meanwhile.* One suffers from duration as the brief intervals recur. One, in dream after dream, quests after an *arena,* no—an *area,* no—an *aura,* no—an *Ur* circumnavigated by a plow. >

One prefers a third option to fight or flight, even one that does not rhyme. One is *grave-grasped,* recalling the unmediated monotony, the *hush* of the planchette's felt footings as they slip over the antique spirit board. One's gaze lingers upon the glaze. One by one the facets of a prime number glint and flare. One sets a weatherworn stone onto the cairn's off-kilter yet underlying balance. One attends to symmetry, begins again the endgame.

17

Weather spills over. The chart, flawed and partial, intimates what remains hidden: a seemingly empty background, or a parable that starts, *A certain man had two sons. . . .* The single window frames a drama not yet disarmed, not yet detonated. The present, ever-vanishing, inflicts an urgent ennui, makes of desire a fulcrum on which disappointment tips, a game whose rules are neither intuited nor articulated, yet adhered to. A master of *indefinition,* one admits that all one's most intimate memories are from movies. Said aloud, in one's own voice and not that of the actor's, the lines seem merely the synopsis of a haiku.

18

Alone, one is preoccupied with one's aloneness. It comes as a revelation. A split-second fractures along its many faults. Smoke, unattached from its match, unwinds as an elusive alchemical proof. Within a taut knot: a sacred space. Having entered the penumbra, one disinters a buried narrative, a notation of incidents and thought. The depicted pictorial space, however, makes no sense.

The sky, like a rare blue glaze first brought forth through maritime trade, and the moon, an imperfect pearl, are all one has ever known of ocean depths. Alone, landlocked beneath charted quadrants, one is at home here, where the future unfurls: a text-inscribed ribbon from an angel's falcon beak, a run-on sentence.

19

In the manner of the great explorers, one is prone to directional ambiguity. Disoriented, not lost, one allows the specifications and advisements to have priority over the territory. At the limits of a language's lucidity, one finds both enactment and enchantment. One finds an ornate chariot preserved in volcanic ash. One finds a heart of five lotuses. Like Odysseus, one wears the dirt and rags of abdication. The boat, carved from pumice, floats on a methane sea. One arrives at an archipelago adorned in distances.

20

To think, one looks up slightly and off to the side: there where contradictions remain unreconciled: a *haze* one calls the distant ochers. One resides in thought and thought is residue.

21

Water subsides and one forgets the tension of surfaces. Still, one keeps notes, not a journal per se, but when a scrap of paper and a pencil coincide infrequently. The landscape remains portioned by clouds and mists, not >

seen *through* the glass, but *in* its reflection. It is still years before a mass grave is discovered beneath the stadium's playing field, before the conjured nits of history are excised from the textbooks, before the fragile work is on view again (illuminated for thirty seconds at a time when a coin is dropped into the slot) after the long and exhaustive restoration. One travels light. Light itself is a kind of companion at one's side. Who has not been guilty now and then of a phototropic attraction? A poem is the work of joinery, not the incidents of rain that are the river, here and elsewhere. Not the grind of gravel and silt. Not the bloom of acidic greens. One navigates the negative space. One says something about the suspicious package and soon regrets doing so. Two hundred thousand Americans dead today from the [ ]. Early fall. Vague weather stalls above the house. Ghosts are driven from the house, but they are not what haunted it. The perspective is only slightly forced, as if an *unknot* were not a knot at all, but absence outlined, or encompassed: a *nobody*, an *antibody*. A looter, amid a swirl of looters, stands still, confused about just what to take and what to leave behind. How to erase, how to nullify the trace when the mnemonic has worked so effectively? *The Covid19 Daily Health Check*, which one must fill out each day online if one plans to go to campus anytime during the semester, asks each day about any *new confusion*. One always answers *no*, but in all honesty cannot tell the new confusion from the old.

22

One has a memory of the voyage—that time evening and daylight coincided (their inherent instability held up by friction). At times, contingent imperatives displace such recollection, and one feels tender toward the upheaval. Behind: a dangerous passage, each penciled word in the diary stitched over with black thread, an orphaned text repurposed as a caption that in no way illumines its image. The obscured window is squeegeed clean, even if too late in the siege. Who sent the invitation? Who left the door ajar?

23

What blessing is not tardy? One consults the oracle: a lost ax foretells a cold winter; a lotus roots in muddy water; even as one watches, a vine coils, rises, and extends; no breeze; no unseen snake through the grasses; a brood of hills along the horizon disrupts the radio signal; like dust, hours accumulate unnoticed, yet one feels the itch and chafe of each minute; the cicadas, not yet emerged, twitch in each shovelful of torpid red clay; the flood plain—jade white—is as bright as the moon until clouds obscure the moon; one is tempted by tangents, but cautious of beginnings.

24

Late, one considers how the roots gnarl around the stone's resistance, how the mycelial network threads beneath the forest floor. A net, or is it a sieve, for memory? One catches up with oneself—a final seal is broken, and silence follows, the silence carefully curated to appear impromptu. The grisaille—still life objects in a sparse tableau—reflects in a gray mirror. Prayers linger above an altar, altered by the sacrifice. A spider repairs >

the woven cosmos. How can any act not prefigure death? Shame is part of it, which constricts like an invasive vine. One did not follow the cautionary tale, stitched together with splinters and nettle, thus read each page as *allegory* rather than *depiction*. Beyond the scrapyards and power station: the cruciform arrangement of the rivers as in paradise. As if to refute the linear, one repurposes the castoffs as counterweights, the in-between as the *not-quite-appearing*, as the *not-quite-disappearing*.

25

One had hoped to contain multitudes, but one, it turns out, is only one.

26

A compass steps into curvature, pivots around a fixed point and, as it is drawn closed, encloses. At odds with their hours: shadows. Worn bent broom straws leave a trail of grit, unresolved without terminus. The hinge, opened or closed, is a coda, a prime indivisible by itself. One marks time beside still waters. The past lurks. Ghosts of the recent past linger—a spectral coterie. One enters in the midst of a story an ongoing-ness, its arcades and facades out of step with fashion, its realism depleted and disrupted by a man and angel wrestling, by affliction and deliverance.

27

One looks for a loophole but finds a noose. One observes but has no intent of rendering the clarity or the concealment. One mirrors theory and, in theory, mirrors. One is a brief incarnation. One has slipped into namelessness. In lieu of flowers, one sends a telegraph. And by way of the telegraph: regrets.

28

Beneath attendant weather, one surveys the changing landscape, the routines of isolation. With a stick of carbonized willow, one renders clouds, the wooded edge in headlight glare, the notations and marks to document the dance for future reference, the dance one calls *being-looked-at.* One affixes an image in the dark. One misreads *stain* as *satin,* mistakes the echo's underside for the flux of reflection. One unwinds horsehair from a cocklebur; strews salt in a furrow. One finds the false Romanticism no less attractive than the more authentic kind. One distinguishes among ambiguities. The granary is full of wind, the linguistic phenomena of silence. The façade's exterior is scaffolded. One has the ability to modularize complex systems, if those systems happen to be poems. At a slender threshold of birches and sky, one does not intrude but eavesdrops. Lacking a straight man, one shrugs.

29

Without any archival impulse, without a longing to uncover, as with a scalpel, the cause, or to immure some ancient flicker amid the silvery expanse of stars, one notices the capacity of objects to disrupt space: the unanticipated element absent from the periodic table, the toppled statues, the humid air thick with roofer's tar. Something like normalcy persists, but as always does >

not remedy estrangement, the plotless accumulation of minutes, the viscous, milky surface of memory as thoughts waver or take flight—contingent notations. Wildfires go unchecked in the exclusion zone and move at the wind's will. One longs for the lull of a Flemish still life one moment and the next *pleasure mixed with dread.* One is a squatter in this place, both pilgrim and trespasser. One awaits (what can one do?) other signs from the *Book of Plagues:* parahelios, an onslaught of locusts, or a monsoon of blood rain.

30

The ephemera are neither curated nor preserved. The question is always of time. Of course, the tourniquet, contorted like an ampersand, did not fit. One lacks a mordant to fix the dye. One lacks a braid of serpents. Unused nouns gather dust. What one possesses is improvisation and control, a language awaiting an invitation. But how often one is duped, hoodwinked. How often the gallery is closed for installation. Uncouth clouds conceal open ground. The ready-made is made, perhaps, but not ready. In a grotto along the coastline, one finds a prayer wrapped in surgical gauze, a shelter stitched from moth-light.

31

One has an inkling. As if augury were performed with an auger, one feels the prick and turn of premonition, knowing full well that déjà vu is an experience of simultaneity, the perception of perception as it is perceived, recollected the instant it is collected, without the distances of memory. Still, one feels a shiver, feels pins and needles as one recognizes—no—experiences the *now* as foretold, as a fated destination. Above one, each star is still moored to a past.

32

The immediate past, scuffed and smudged as it is with chalk, stippled and hatched with ink, weathers, wears out. At the maple's base, the urinous stink of a thousand cicada carcasses. Fallen wings glitter surfaces. One had hoped to eschew the documentary impulse, the forensic attention to detail. Depressed at mid-summer, one broods. A poem is site specific. The scale is one inch to a mile. The whole sky fits on the surface of a puddle. One listens: a single chirr, a bit lower, a bit slower than the general drone and din.

33

Is it immediacy or reflection one longs for in a diaristic form? Or perhaps a sensation similar to ambling? One can unstitch with a snip flames from a burning archive. One is prone to a prescient sensitivity. One receives coins for cans at the redemption center, yet feels forlorn, feral: a forsaken gurney beneath rain in a forest clearing. Look: a rotting stump collapsing in upon itself where the Tree of Life once stood. There at the lace-edge of memory. One composes a landscape, delights in the endless possibility of a single sheet of graph paper. The moment, inconspicuous in its brevity, is tethered to fog. This is the hour the window loses all transparency. Nothing can outdistance the past as it accelerates and retreats. >

34

A light is kept on all night in an empty room, and, on the other side of the house, one can hear the shimmer of the filament, an image as it emerges from silver and selenium. One takes a step back: lets the committee revise the paragraph; lets the backlash backfire. One is a Mesmer without mojo, without a hint or a glimmer. One occupies the horizontal, leaves the vertical to gods and devils, birds and grubs. The dub is out of sync. The escapement's anchor releases. Then it snags. What is violence depleted of urgency? One feels free, without hindrance. One feels jilted, without recourse. Without a hint, one recalls the room's obsolete utility. One sets a riddle—both a lure and a cage—as one sets a trap.

35

Attention elsewhere, one does not read but holds the book open, looks down intently at each blank page, but cannot seem to make one's eyes move left to right without moving one's head. The shroud, unwoven each night, is shuttle-rubbed, dark and oily from touch. Day arrives as elusory shifts of light, as cloud totems. Home again postponed by detours. To dictate direction, one applies a bird to an uncluttered bit of blue. One draws smoke in the distance with candle soot ink. One has a bag of assorted seeds as evidence of the journey's distances. An adept, one slept in an orchard of nooses. One recognizes the partiality of any single attempt and refrains (meaning both *to cease* and *to once again*). One affixes a lens of ice to a *camera obscura* and documents the chaste dryness of a snakeskin, the threshold of a tenuous space. As sea levels rise, the continent becomes contingent. What is seduction without desire? Each tone, impression, and aberration: the worth and weight of thistledown. One has only oneself to blame, although there are others who come in a close second.

36

How tiring becoming has become—the state of emergence, the degrees of visibility, the despite and because of. *As onto the loaded present,* as Valery says. One lives on the surface of the Earth, walks a leaf-strewn track through a forest where diffuse sunlight distorts time. One wears primitive camouflage against facial recognition software. One rehearses the future but cannot keep up with the script changes. Artificial intelligence encroaches upon sacred geometry. The sulfur vents vent sulfur. A pilgrim steps from a briar tangle. Like fire, one is born of two sticks, a spark that catches and must be fed.

37

While the GPS recalculates, one becomes a resemblance. What one is experiencing is not time travel or teleportation, but a tone generated within the ear itself, which one associates with the presence of an undetected third party. One fast-forwards to the catastrophe. The impurities are skimmed. The databases over-mined. The stitch of memory is concealed. Entrusted with disease, one endures it. When science and metaphysics were not separate disciplines, one had an easier go of it. The August meteor showers are breath-taking; still someone in the crowd finds it necessary to read the >

subtitles aloud. Stumbles over multisyllabic words. The names of constellations. Masked, one rebreathes one's breath, becomes ingrown, a carbon dump. Is shame a side effect of desire, one wonders, or is it the other way around? Mold darkens the toppled wheat. Fate is woven on a jerry-rigged loom.

38

Wherever one stands, the voice-over assures, is sacred land. The scavenged-for clues are elusive. To get a better view, one stands on rain-stained cinderblocks. One is given a lexicon of erasures, a drift of clouds as coordinates. After eons of erosion, the familiar becomes invisible. One must squat to peer through the peephole, thus is quick to give the next person a turn. Like a scene of torture: a bell hung upside down with rope by its clapper.

39

One steers clear of theory, but the airbags deploy nonetheless as the car careens into the ditch. Then, one must follow the path within the story-within-the-story. A fallen tree bridges a stream in the boulder-strewn meadow. One climbs uphill toward houselights and finds laundry pinned on the line frozen. Knocks on the door. The cold and damp penetrate. The memory of it all is semi-transparent: a long stretch of spring that is, in fact, winter. One embraces ambiguity like a Harlow monkey.

40

A line can divide and enclose a space. A reflection

darkens the water. In the end, it is all busywork. When one's mind races like this, whiskey helps. And after that: a little three-lined verse that follows the prose to cleanse the palate. Winter is the only season to keep its covenant. One notices that the pollarded trees look like archaic crutches. The paint is faintly brighter where the picture once hung. When the ancestors return, they speak a different language; they talk willingly, without bribe or sacrifice, but one cannot understand a word they say.

41

One is alarmed by the reciprocal gaze. The devil, preoccupied, has no use for one's idle hands. What else might one see on holiday? A waterfall spill and expand, tangle and fray before the mist and splash? A snake hoarding pearls in its nest? A stain dispersed? A window bricked in? A shadow pinned to a wall? A beloved pined after? A series of vignettes? A blue tarp over a linden branch as a rude screen? A fiddlehead uncoil? A nascent fascism? A view up from under ice? A beautiful in-law? One stands out in the crowd. With each step forward, the feedback enlarges.

42

Not fresh snow, but morning light upon the snow: white tulle, a gesso of marble dust and rabbit skin glue, a poverty of blues. One writes with one's right hand and erases with one's left. Soon the left becomes the dominant hand, as strong as it is sinister. Spring and summer pass: a diet of fears, a disorder of acute angles. The something borrowed turns out to be something >

remembered: a cathedral of trees, say, or the emptiness of clear glass. Although clouds of algae muddled the surface, the bottom (although the focus is faulty) is just about discernible. One sends one's greeting from elsewhere on a postcard. One recalls the fall of the last great dynasty as if it were yesterday. Perhaps it was.

43

One must construct a distance from which to see. A rock here. A tree there. One aspires to an archaism by way of Giotto. Wilderness consumes the city. Wilderness gives way to an ice age. One recalls draped figures in a shelter. Cart tracks. A deserted gravel pit flooded with light. The poem is an archive of indecisions. The horizon, bisected by smoke, is no more or less. One tries to stay put but takes the long way around. One has reached an entropic juncture and has only a grain doll as an offering.

44

Onc can end where one began without enacting a circle, but a circle does please with its symmetry. Of course, the treaties go unheeded. Even now, the wind finds the prairie melancholy. A through line divides and crosses out. The pond is low in its basin, stagnant, but its depths will not settle. One would not have imagined the dark ocean-like passage, the muteness of grass, or the phone booth's inevitable obsolescence. One pounces the image through the pin-pricked paper with powdered charcoal onto the plaster wall, but the outline smears and seems to be merely what it is: a tracing of sorts, a copy. Dusk is not even dense yet in the treetops when Death arrives as a black swan.

45

Can one's interiority be both vast and cramped at once? One has suffered from what Keats would call an *unslumberous night.* The shorelines will soon be submerged and the rivers silt-laden. The story still must pass through many hands, but one prepares for the telling and the retelling, the hearing and again the hearing. How to ignite from the melting tundra a spark? How to shoo the mountain of flies from the thawing mastodon? Is an echo latent prior to a sounding? Tomorrow recedes from the field of vision. Between restlessness and sleep, one is both the horse and its fallen rider.

46

One has spent the morning with a small child who has taken to forming one's own words a split-second or less after one has spoken. The echo is unnerving. An echo does not emit but absorbs time. The conversation (although it is not that at all) feels rehearsed. How much of the depths are filled with jettisoned ballast? That vortex of gulls—does it ascend or descend?

47

One is invited to get the birds out of the attic, but instead unstuffs the insulation from between joists, overturns the hope chest, gets contrails entangled among the cirrus. One arrives in spite of all the mileposts missing from the river road. One listens to John Lee Hooker play "Don't Look Back," and thinks of Orpheus in the underworld. How often does one have to watch the assassin screw the >

silencer silently on, his breath held as the door inches open? As respite from the real, one courts simulation. What is the material of mirage? One prefers a footstool to a precipice, asperity to a celadon glaze. One recalls Albuquerque as muted sand and rose tones. *Sunlight on a pine plank,* one says, recalling the inherent light and luminosity. One traces an afterthought and finds in its place the torn rag of a hornets' nest. One has kept count and today there are 700,000 Americans dead from the [ ]. One's memory is shopworn. Abraded. Or rather one's memories are. To be given one's druthers—that must be what one wants. The eraser does not erase, but smears, smudges, leaves visible areas of damage, of alteration.

48

Was it grief or grievance that consumed one? The current ferment? The isolated incidents of the quarantine? One hammers a nail. Lights a candle. Lets each stand in for prayer. *I can only note that the past is beautiful,* Virginia Woolf writes, *because one never realizes an emotion at the time. It expands later, and thus we don't have complete emotions about the present, only about the past.* One occupies a moment suspended between events. Radiance is a side effect. The little bell at the front desk lures, but one resists the temptation to ring it. Displeased with the accommodations, one accommodates oneself and feels finally at home. Or at least for now comfortable. Perhaps in memory the room will have a view. The canal's backward S all mother of pearl beneath a tarnished moon's silver.

49

One's fate is written on an oak leaf in a swirl of oak leaves. One is on a parallel journey between figments and meanders. A dream is a diorama of sorts—reconstituted, inhabitable, but in no way a shelter. The elevated vantage point eliminates the horizon, which is mired, of course, in nostalgia. One comes out of the wilderness. One brings along a grid to tame the indeterminate space. Water diverges around the rocks. Given time, the water wears away at the rock. After a storm, the trees reclaim their nonchalance. *Tell me, how did you feel when you come out the wilderness, come out the wilderness, come out the wilderness? Tell me, how did you feel when you come out the wilderness, leaning on the Lord?*

50

One reads through a magnifying glass the lace's latticed intricacy, the veil as a text of ambiguity. How a thread tethers and repairs. One has been at times *willfully blind.* At other times *short-sighted.* One offers voids, illusions of transparency, a stage before the actors have entered. One is not blameless, but close enough. As the forest claims a position in the foreground, one is between lucidity and indeterminacy. One is in the midst a dark wood, a *selva oscura.*

ACKNOWLEDGMENTS

Works included here have appeared in the following journals and anthologies. I am most grateful for the kind and careful attention offered by the editors who first supported and offered a home to these various writings, most often, in earlier forms:

Adroit, American Journal of Poetry, American Life in Poetry, American Voice, Arkansas International, Book of Matches, Carolina Quarterly, Cimarron Review, Cincinnati Review, Copper Nickel, december, Diagram, Diode, The Disquieting Muse, Divot, Elsewhere, Figure One, Georgia Review, Gettysburg Review, Good River Review, Gris-Gris, Image, Iowa Journal of Literary Studies, I-70 Review, Laurel Review, Lost Pilots Lit, Manoa, Metafore, Miracle Monocle, Natural Bridge, Newfound, New World Writing, Phantom Drift, Poetry International, Proem, Rhino, 2River Review, Southern Poetry Review, Southwest Review, Sou'wester, Superpresent, Talking River, Terrain, This Is What America Looks Like, Two Hawks Quarterly, and *Wildness.*

The Future Perfect: A Fugue was selected by John Yau as the winner of the Snowbound Chapbook Award and published by Tupelo Press in 2022. Many thanks to John Yau and all the good people at Tupelo Press.

DEDICATIONS

The following poems are dedicated as follows:

"The Dress" for Allison Funk

"A Weathered Ladder" for Gwen Strauss

"Pocketsize Notebook with a Black Elastic Strap to Hold It Closed" for H. L. Hix

"The River Still Ragged with Ice Floes" for Jason Sommer

"Recently Recovered Pages from the Complete List of Everything" for Jeff Hamilton

"Ash-Grit" for Jennifer Atkinson

"From the Get-Go" for Andy Cox

"As in Any Marriage" for Andy Fogle

"The Old Devil in the Tree" for Brian Barker

"To No One in Particular" for Roger Lathbury

"Last Radio Playing" for Martin Mitchell

"Another World Afloat on Fire" for Steve Schreiner

"A Large Expanse of Glass Set upon Twin Sawhorses" for Doug Luman

"Some Will Tell You Their Secrets"
for Anna Catherine Del Valle

"Yet the Past Hardly Existed" for Peter Streckfus

"The History of the Siege" for Sally Keith

Deep thanks to Ian Cappelli for many fun, rich, and illuminating conversations about the art of the prose poem while some of the poems in this book were being written.

NOTES

The phrase in "The Afterlife" "the secure tranquility of simple and ingenious things" is borrowed from Franz Roh's "Post-expressionism: Magical Realism: Problems of the Newest European Painting" (1925).

"Lilith" is an ekphrasis in response to Kiki Smith's "Lilith" (1994) at the Metropolitan Museum of Art.

"Shallow Ford in the River" riffs on a passage from Yoshida Kenko's *Essays in Idleness* written between 1330 and 1332.

"The Old Devil in the Tree" is the title of a collage by artist and poet Brian Barker.

The statement by John Cage in "Novel Microbes in the Ice Melt" is from his *Silences* (1961).

The Bob Dylan song mentioned in "Last Radio Playing" is "Shooting Star" from *Oh Mercy* (1989).

"The Weight" epigraph is from the song of the same title by The Band on the album *Music from Big Pink* (1968).

"Gates Swung Open One after Another" is a translation/version/variation in prose of Du Fu's poem "P'eng-ya Road" that I attempted in graduate school in the early 1980s. I have whittled the draft back recently to its current elegiac mode without having consulted the original or my notes from back then. Marvin Bell was my teacher at the time at The Iowa Writers' Workshop and a dear friend thereafter.

>

The Roland Barthes statement in "On the Fulcrum of *Of*" is from *The Pleasure of the Text* (1973).

The idea of an elegy as a *tomb* in "I'm Gonna Run to the City of Refuge" is borrowed, of course, from Stephane Mallarme. When I have found myself standing in the need of prayer, Blind Willie Johnson's *The Complete Blind Willie Johnson* (1993) has been the hymnal and prayer book to which I turn for solace over the past thirty years.

In "Repeat-to-Fade," the Federico Garcia Lorca poem mentioned is "Death." Larry Levis was my teacher at both the University of Missouri at Columbia and The Iowa Writers' Workshop. His kindness and generosity to me, a stumbling novice, still amazes me.

In "The Future Perfect: A Fugue," the phrase "an invitation of ether and stars" echoes Charles Baudelaire in "The Voyage" (1861). Willa Cather's words are from *The Song of the Lark* (1915).

"Oblique Strategies" borrows its title from a card-based method developed in 1975 by Brian Eno and Peter Schmidt for promoting creativity.

In "The History of the Siege," the references include: 29: "pleasure mixed with dread" is Immanual Kant's phrase; 36: Paul Valery, *Collected Works, Volume II, Poems in the Rough* (2016); 45: John Keats, "Endymion" (1818); 48: *The Diary of Virginia Woolf, volume three* (1981); 49: "Come Out the Wilderness" is an African-American Spiritual, the first written documentation of which is in 1895.

ADDITIONAL PRAISE FOR HISTORY OF THE SIEGE

Eric Pankey's *The History of the Siege* is prose poetry deeply faithful to the European roots of the genre, resurrected from the *ennui* of pandemic and the horror of a recent tyranny, where, as he writes, "the slow art of forgetting occupies what passes here for time." Some pieces recall the landscape of Rimbaud's *Season of Hell,* where the father is cast as fire breather and the mother the artist whose cigarettes set the house on fire; others are reminiscent of Max Jacob's dreams, or his "The Cock and the Pearl" from Jacob's seminal volume, *The Dice Cup.* In Pankey's achievement those Jacobian reveries are, to my eye, the most marvelous reinventions of the form, masterfully translated within a twenty-first century vocabulary. In "Recently Recovered Pages from *The Complete List of Everything*" and in the title poem (a kind of book that closes the book), the intelligence, language, and imagery are nothing short of breathtaking: "Like Odysseus, one wears the dirt and rags of abdication... One arrives at an archipelago adorned in distances." *The History of the Siege* not only holds but advances Eric Pankey's reputation as one of the best poets writing in English today. This work is spectacular.

—DAVID KEPLINGER

The History of the Siege navigates intimate topographies of memory, grief, shame, and yearning. A lucid voyage of clarity, depth, and ineffable wonder, Pankey's poems assert their humanity, courage, and faith in a difficult world. His language treads ambivalent territories where spirituality and mortality intersect. There, a vast mind lives. Such meditations gather into a profound frieze of life itself, sweeping across the precision of childhood to the stinging battlefield of Covid 19. Of history and the >

self, Pankey notes, "Ghosts are driven from the house, but they are not what haunted it." Like water, fire, air, memory and earth, these prose poems gather elementally into a revelatory force.

—RACHEL ELIZA GRIFFITHS

"The question," Eric Pankey avows in his serial title poem, "is always of time." An "archive of indecisions," *The History of the Siege* is a beguiling book of inventories and elegies, of fugue and fever dream, of uncanny conundrums and para-fairy tales, in which doors open onto doors leading up to "a balcony that steps off into fog." Each prose poem is a Pandora's box whose contents exceed the frame, as we freefall through detours of improv and control. A mix of wild, associative capaciousness with forensic exactitude, these "firings" are actually fueled—not foiled—by distorted signals and radio delay, interference, odd code, feedback loops and loopholes, "glitchy disharmony." By Pankey's hypnagogic logic, any experience that's out of sync, from pandemic panic to déjà vu, is the proper sign of our times. And what time is it anyway, what tense are we even in, when "the boat's wake arrives before the boat"—?

—ANDREW ZAWACKI